The Advisor Playbook

By Duncan MacPherson and Chris Jeppesen

Edited by Michael M. Lane

Acknowledgements

We'd like to thank our families for putting up with the hours spent on assembling this book, our co-workers for their support, ideas and suggestions and, most importantly, all the professional advisors we've worked with over the years.

Your input and responses, the issues and concerns you've brought forward or helped spark solutions for, are the driving factor and most vital resource in the evolution of these practice management processes and the underlying laws that govern them.

About the Authors

Thank you for seeing the merit in acquiring this book. We appreciate that your time is valuable and we view it as a tremendous compliment and responsibility that you are investing your time to better understand our approach and process.

Let us tell you a little about ourselves:

About Duncan MacPherson

I am the CEO of Pareto Systems, a practice management and business development consulting firm dedicated to improving the productivity of professional advisors. I've spent the last 20 years traveling the world speaking at conferences and coaching top performers on how to deploy a process that will unlock their full potential personally and professionally.

Along with my team of coaches, I have developed and refined several one-to-one consulting programs including The Pareto System, The Fee-worthy Advisor, Succession 360 and the Advisor Flight Plan. I've also collaborated with enterprise clients to create one-to-many solutions, including train-the-trainer approaches.

I've invested those experiences into a philosophy that says stewardship is more attractive than salesmanship, and a process that makes implementation predictable and sustainable. My goal is that you can translate that into results using this *Playbook*.

I live in Kelowna, British Columbia, Canada. You can find me on LinkedIn at ca.linkedin.com/in/duncanmacpherson.

About Chris Jeppesen

I am the Head of Advisory Practices at First Trust, a firm known not only for its robust investment product line which includes UITs, ETFs, SMAs and VAs (to name a few), but also for its commitment to the growth of financial advisors. First Trust has dedicated many years to finding (and investing in) creative ways to help financial advisors grow their practices.

As the Head of Advisory Practices, my goal over the last 18 years has been to give financial advisors the tools to develop an efficient business model focused on building long-term client trust and loyalty. First Trust has helped develop this model through a broad range of investment, advisory and management solutions and I am proud that First Trust has been nationally recognized for this solution-based approach.

The Advisor Playbook is the culmination of my years of practice management and seeing financial advisors achieve success through these proven methods and strategies.

There is - sometimes - an I in Team

As we collaborated on this book, one issue that kept getting in the way was alternating from I to we. While we both have many shared experiences working together with professional advisors, we each have many more encounters where we individually worked with an advisory team to unlock higher levels of productivity. That said, we made the decision to present this book as a single voice. To us it seems to flow more smoothly and is more conversational.

Editor's Preface

Practice management is often misunderstood.

It's confused with marketing, or is limited to strategizing about branding, or simply seen as old-school salesmanship.

Practice management is how you build an organized toolbox of all your processes – branding, marketing, service activities, core functions – and constantly tune and keep that toolbox efficient and effortless. It's a network of interrelated skills, processes and strategies that build value in a business while making it manageable, scalable and ensuring the owner runs the business and not the other way around.

Duncan MacPherson and Pareto Systems have been in the forefront of practice management in the realm of the professional advisor for a quarter-century. Chris Jeppesen brings his own decades of professional knowledge to the table. The processes in this book have grown over those years, through constant refinement and improvement. They'll help you to perform that same refinement and improvement on your business, and regain liberation and order in your personal and professional life.

As you progress through the book, you'll realize that each process is implemented in synergy with every other. Referrals are influenced by your service which is influenced by your process, which is influenced by your philosophy, which is influenced by your ideal client definition, life and business goals. Nothing exists in a vacuum, and everything is, in the end, focused on a single unwavering goal: To build real, advocate relationships with your ideal clients that will generate both growth through referrals and the capacity for that growth.

How you are perceived is key in every step of that circle, and readers who take on board what the *Playbook* outlines will come away with an understanding of how they are perceived, how to cast themselves as a consultant with a process rather than a salesperson with a quota, and will set a constantly rising bar for their own success.

You'll be amazed at how common-sense most of the processes and strategies seem, and probably horrified at how often you've wandered from the path or failed to implement them due to a lack of clarity or simple distraction.

I envy the first-time reader the feeling of enlightenment that comes as you grasp the central tenets of this book, and the anticipation that comes from having an actionable plan and process that makes going to work a positive experience, and a positive investment.

Michael Lane, September, 2015

Contents

Section 4: Professionalize the Client Experience 111

Organizing Yourself and Your Clients

Section 5: Refer-ability 169

Being Attractive to Your Ideal Clients

What You Can Expect to Implement Using This Playbook

Before beginning, I want to give you a look at the end.

With your "Why" clear, and after absorbing "How" to put each process in motion, readers will come away from the *Playbook* with the following firmly in place. You can expect to:

- **Reach clarity on your branding**, make it memorable, clear and an effective tool to attract potential clients.

- **Build a plan to win** through design rather than luck. You will analyze your gaps and untapped opportunities and use them to chart a course forward.

- **Create a documented procedures manual** to make your business run like a Swiss watch, whether you are in the office or not.

- **Define your ideal client** and communicate that knowledge to rainmakers and clients to focus referrals of consistent quality.

- **Utilize Triple-A segmentation** to optimize your results. You will invest your time with those clients who are the best fit for you, and who provide the greatest ROI and satisfaction.

- **Be seen as a consultant with a process** rather than a salesperson with a product. Your focus will be on stewardship, and your clients will understand and appreciate the value you provide to them.

- **Build competitor-proof relationships** with your top clients by gathering and utilizing F.O.R.M. information.

- **Right-size your practice and increase its value**, while simultaneously regaining liberation and order in your life.

- **Prepare to be the advisor of the future**, as demographics and technologies evolve.

- **Build measurable value in your business** for the future, whether for succession or eventual sale.

- **Learn why done is better than perfect** and avoid procrastination. You will make process your driving force, and learn to avoid the pitfall of diminishing intent.

When you finish the *Playbook*, revisit this list. I want you to look at where you were, where you are, and where you are headed with the clarity that comes from knowledge paired with action.

Section 1: Let's Get Started

A Primer for the Professional Advisor

When the why is clear, the how is easy - Jim Rohn

Starting with Action

To start, you must act.

The practice and relationship management strategies contained in this section – even if all you initially do is read this chapter – will fast-track you to results. They will move you beyond being seen as a salesperson with a quota to a more attractive space where you are perceived as a professional consultant with a valuable stewardship service. You should continue into the meat of this book to drill down, polish and perfect your process, but I want you to hit the ground running with the tools in hand to start seeing immediate results.

As you work your way through the *Playbook*, you'll find actionable, implementable processes that will build loyalty and advocacy among your ideal clients, attract more ideal clients and referrals going forward and build the value of your business while reducing your stress and regaining control and liberation in your life.

You may be asking a question right now: Does the world need another book on practice management and client acquisition? Hasn't everything been said when it comes to professionalizing the client experience and growing a business? I have read countless books over the years on these topics, and most have provided similar and often familiar insights.

Why this book? What are the key points of difference and what can you expect from it that will make reading it a good investment of your time and money?

Two words come to mind: Process and implementation.

The Power of Process

This book is not a collection of tips, ideas and concepts. It is a collection of proven strategies, of processes that have been refined and formatted into structured procedures. As you read through these pages, I will also be talking about many immutable laws and principles that affect us all in business and in life, and the way to use process to make the most of the positive and minimize the negative.

We have to respect these laws, or we will pay the price.

One of my favorites is the *Law of Diminishing Intent*. Over the years, how many ideas have you been exposed to that resonated with you initially, but then went to your head to die? Ideas alone are interesting, but can have the lasting value of an energy drink. A *process* is far more powerful than an idea because you can get your head around it and imagine, clearly, how it can apply to your unique situation. That understanding is half the equation; the remainder is implementation.

You've heard the old saying, "After all is said and done, more is often said than done." A lot is said in books, seminars and consulting programs. Ideas are discussed, but processes are *implemented* and that implementation is what translates into results. Every aspect of this book has been written around actionable processes that you can apply to your business to make meaningful and measurable progress.

All of which begs the question: What is the origin of these processes? I get a lot of credit from people who buy into this approach. They applaud me for being creative because of how the processes have been structured and presented. Truth be told, I'm not creative. What I am is a master assimilator. After many years of consulting directly with some of the most professional and productive people in financial services, insurance, accounting, legal and countless other knowledge-for-profit fields, I've observed commonalities that separate the best from the rest.

Rather than report that knowledge to you as concepts and success stories, they are presented as processes that you can personalize and execute on with predictability. Think about it. You can go to Wikipedia and find countless ideas, but finding a playbook that has processes that are *actionable* rather than *abstract* is a completely different experience.

I used the phrase "knowledge for profit" deliberately in the *Playbook*. This book has been framed specifically for professionals who think for a living. Your services are *transmitted* rather than *transported*. Some people run businesses that build and sell tangible things, and the client experience can be more transactional. Others provide services and, in many cases, the client relationship can be ongoing.

For a professional whose solutions are not tangible, and the benefits of which can be delayed, it is essential to create a client experience that de-commoditizes your services.

A Playbook Makes Taking Action Predictable

Let me provide some context on two essential drivers of this book: The origins and the philosophy embodied within it.

My philosophy is simple. A client relationship should be started and maintained through stewardship rather than salesmanship.

Salespeople ask you to buy something. They have customers who fixate on products, pricing and performance. Salespeople are motivated by immediate commissions rather than long-term commitment and, essentially, they are trading their time for money. They aren't building anything of durable value.

A consultant asks a client to buy into something long-term and those relationships are connected by an aligned philosophy, planning strategy and process. As I'll repeat on *many* occasions in this book, your solutions should be bought, not sold.

The origins of our processes have grown and been constantly tuned over years of consulting with professional advisors. It's been an organic process of assimilation, as I said. Learning what separates the best from the rest and finding systemic ways to implement those habits as processes for knowledge-for-profit professionals has been a fulfilling and fascinating career.

Some of the most fulfilling and revealing aspects of our client interactions have stemmed from our Business Evaluation Process. This is a gap analysis where I pop the hood on someone's business in order to make specific observations about their untapped opportunities, overlooked vulnerabilities and the unaddressed issues that could be undermining them. It's a way to get clarity on the issues specific to a given business and begin to build that all-important playbook. It helps the business owner kick their own tires and get a fresher, clearer sense of the state of the business and the trajectory it's on.

Find the Gaps and Fill Them

The format I use in our gap analysis is straightforward, and it's a tool you should keep close at hand whenever you do planning. It lets you dig into the three key drivers of your business:

Your Core Solutions Process: These are the products and services you provide and how they are delivered to differentiate and de-commoditize you.

Your Practice Management Process: This is the degree to which you and your team have professionalized the client experience with best practices.

Your Relationship Management Process: This encompasses your overall communications and branding strategy, focused on ensuring that clients and prospective clients understand and appreciate your value.

As you know by now, this book is called *The Advisor Playbook*. I've referred to it as a "playbook" because it will guide you through methodically cracking the code to consistent client acquisition and an impeccable client experience; of becoming a consultant with a process rather than a salesperson with a quota.

"Cracking the code" is inspired by the three components I just mentioned. I think of them as three numbers in a combination lock and - if you dial in all three in the right sequence - you can achieve a breakthrough. Metaphors aside, when I conduct a Business Evaluation Process, this is where I start, and the process generally reveals the following strengths and gaps for a typical professional:

Core Solutions Process: 8 out of 10

Practice Management Process: 6 out of 10

Relationship Management Process: 4 out of 10

Initially, this process is designed to provide clarity to the business professional. They don't require drastic, wholesale changes to the way they conduct themselves. Often, it's minor adjustments that can lead to major improvements, and the most dramatic results are usually found in the realms of practice- and relationship-management.

This is especially important for someone who has plateaued – life and business are good, but surely another level can be attained? For others it's about looking beyond any inertia confidence ("Hey, it's worked in the past, why mess with it?") and stepping back to assess the track they are on. Like any journey you embark on, mid-course corrections are often required to offset drift that occurs.

It's all about trajectory. Success is a direction, not a destination.

The best aspect of the Business Evaluation Process, and what contributes strongly to using what is revealed as an actionable critical path going forward, is that it is a Socratic approach.

If you've read anything about Socrates - an original "Man on the Mountain", a guru who was sought out for advice - you know that he rarely gave any. His view was that you can't change someone. You can only make them think. It's the process of critical thinking that can help someone come to their own conclusions, break the status quo and inspire action; action driven by self-motivation rather than a pep talk. With that in mind, the Business Evaluation Process is essentially a series of linked and sequential questions to reveal the issues and key performance indicators that can serve to provide that clarity.

As the issues are revealed, the process starts to make connections to the immutable laws and principles I mentioned earlier. These laws will be woven throughout this book but here is a preview:

- *The Law of Cause and Effect*: It's our activity that determines our productivity.

- *The Law of Attraction*: Salespeople chase new clients, consultants attract them.

- *The Law of Environment*: We are products of our environment; the clients and team members we choose to associate with.

- *The Law of Familiarity:* The more familiar something becomes over time, the more we tend to take it for granted or trivialize its value.

- *The Law of Resonance*: There is a signal-to-noise ratio. Is your message unique and does it resonate, or is it dismissed because it is noise?

- *The Law of Diminishing Intent*: When you are exposed to an idea you feel would positively impact you, you must take action immediately. If you don't, the likelihood that you will ever implement it fades quickly.

- *The Contrast Principal*: Prospective clients contrast you to their existing provider. That is their frame of reference. Is your approach clearly favorable?

There are other laws and principles that I will apply throughout this book but I'd like to look at the *Law of Cause and Effect,* first. If you want to improve your productivity, the best place to start is by examining your activities. Look no further than the Pareto principle, also known as the 80/20 rule. In most cases, about 80 percent of your business stems from about 20 percent of your clients. It makes sense, therefore, that you consistently invest 80 percent of your time – both pro-actively and reactively – on that 20 percent.

It's common sense, but not always common practice.

Many business people reactively spend 80 percent of their time on the 80 percent of their clients who generate 20 percent of the business, and that can contribute to a plateau. Looking deeper, this is a factor that separates the best from the rest. The best don't major in minor things.

The 80/20 rule applies to your usual day, as well. About 80 percent of your productivity comes from roughly 20 percent of your activity. You have 80 percent of your impact every day in about an hour. If you can master what goes into that hour, and compound it over time, getting to the next level is predictable.

It sounds simple, but you must pay close attention to where you allocate your time. Contrary to the old cliché, time is *not* money. Your time is your most valuable commodity and you can easily mistake motion for action.

I see many professional advisors who stay busy for the sake of movement but with little focus on measurable achievement. Engaging, for example, in a marketing campaign for the sake of making a splash, versus building and supporting an incremental branding strategy, just can't compare on many levels. You're trading your time for money but not building anything of value.

In my office is a work of art that features a giant hourglass with the lid popped open. There is a person with a bag of sand over his shoulder pouring more sand into the glass. You'll see it on the cover of this book, because the image is a meaningful one to me. It reminds me that time is flying by and we can't pause and top it up. Legendary business guru Jim Rohn said it best, "You either get *through* the day, or *from* the day."

The best way to get *from* the day is to pro-actively plan it out. Allocate your time and minimize the need or temptation to react to things that can disrupt your momentum. As I get older, the value of time becomes more apparent, because its passage seems to be accelerating (Am I the only person who marvels at the fact that the movie E.T. was released over 30 years ago?)

Throughout this book I will reveal more observations that stem from the Business Evaluations I've performed over the years. They cover areas within all three of the numbers in the "combination lock" and they are presented in an actionable format rooted in a professional philosophy and structured within a process that you and your team can customize.

As a jumping off point, the logical place to start is where I consistently see the most significant gaps; in the areas of professional branding, communication and everything else that goes into your Relationship Management Process. Ultimately, this measures your ability to articulate your value in a way that differentiates and elevates you, so that clients fully understand and appreciate your value and can, in turn, relay it to someone else in a compelling way.

The best way to consistently attract new clients with minimal friction is through referrals from clients and strategic partners. It's far more effective to work with people who are already convinced, and teach them how to convince people on your behalf, than it is to try to convince new people who are unfamiliar with you.

Salespeople look for new clients while consultants are found. Consultants have services that are bought, while salespeople have services that are sold. There is a profound distinction here, and how you start a relationship will have a tremendous impact on its full value over its lifetime, especially when it comes to refer-ability.

Branding is What They Hear

You may be wondering about the sometimes fuzzy distinction between marketing and branding.

Marketing typically involves stand-alone campaigns and strategies that have a beginning and an end. Branding is ongoing and every investment into your professional branding strategy builds upon itself, and can become a proprietary asset over time. Marketing is short-term and branding lasts the course; it just keeps going and gets stronger as time passes. There is an old maxim that states that, "Marketing is what you say, branding is what they hear."

At a basic level, marketing helps you *sell* something, while branding helps you *build* something. In this book you'll find I return to branding time and time again.

As a knowledge-for-profit professional, you have to avoid a commoditized mindset. It's not an initial sale that's key, it's the ongoing relationship. As an example, think of Gillette™. Do they make their money selling you a razor, once? No, it's the ongoing relationship – your attachment to the brand - that keeps you coming back for more blades for your favorite razor, and that's what earns their money.

Marketing is what you say. It's what you convey whether it's at a seminar or on LinkedIn or in your various collateral materials. Branding is what your *clients* say about you to somebody else. It's their interpretation relayed to another person.

Branding is absolutely essential in getting to the next level. It's a consistent thread that is woven through everything you do. It helps you stand out, differentiates you, gets people's attention and helps you be memorable.

Both the way your industry is evolving and the speed at which it is being commoditized contain a host of factors that are emphasizing what you *cost* rather than what you're *worth*. Your ability to articulate your value will ensure your clients understand how you're positioned, and they'll always understand the value you bring to their lives.

If you can't explain something simply you don't understand it well enough yourself – Albert Einstein

---

I don't want to trivialize marketing. If you do retirement seminars, client events, drip marketing or social networking, they can have an impact, but they are far from being an exact science. As the old saying goes, "Half of all marketing is wasted. We just don't know which half." As a result, many business people engage in spray-and-pray marketing campaigns that can set them up for the most brutal emotional outcome of all, *antici-pointment,* a hope that something meaningful will happen, but often with an anticlimactic outcome that is temporary, at best. This is not to say that marketing can't play a role and be tremendously effective. It can and I will discuss it later, but it's essential to focus on your branding and overall relationship management process first.

You are in the knowledge-for-profit business; you think for a living. You're not selling things; you're promoting the promise of the future. This can be abstract to a client. Remember, too, that there are many factors that are out of your control. The magnitude of noise is intense. There are many voices nagging at your clients, creating anxiety and uncertainty, and those voices cause them to look to the future with apprehension instead of anticipation. You have to define yourself, and it starts with articulating your value by establishing the verbal extension of your overall branding strategy.

The Law of Resonance reminds us that we have to continually ensure that a client tunes in your message and tunes out the static of competitors. It's like giving your clients noise-canceling head-phones so they can tune out the environmental noise and tune into your signal to stay connected to you.

What can you assume about the prospective client you're going to meet next? You have to remember that they already have a service provider. That is their frame of reference. The way you articulate your value will instantly activate the *Contrast Principle.*

When they hear your value proposition and the way you articulate your value, you position yourself in their minds as an alternative to their current professional and, done correctly, you create a nagging feeling that you are an upgrade to their present situation. What you want to prompt in their mind are these words: *"Finally, this is what I've been looking for!"*

That internal message activates the self-motivation that propels them to want to do business with you. You don't need to convince them. They come to their own conclusions.

How you articulate your value impacts how you are perceived. You want to be perceived as a consultant with a process, not a broker with an agenda to sell something. You want your clients to fully understand and appreciate your value beyond the performance of the solutions you provide. Furthermore, you want your clients to be aware of your full array of services.

Do your clients understand all that you can do, or do they focus on what you've provided for them up to this point in the relationship? Have you future-paced your clients to help them understand the dynamic and fluid nature of their evolving needs? You need a process to convey to them that - as their lives progress and needs unfold - it is your job to get out in front and put the pieces of the puzzle together. This is how you become indispensable to them, literally for life, and bring them to a point where they will contact you the moment a meaningful event occurs that prompts a new need.

Consistent Communication is a Process

What I'll do now is provide a structured approach to creating and presenting your own value proposition. It is a format that you can follow to take the verbal extension of your branding strategy and professionalize it with a process.

A value proposition is not a data-dumping, jargon-filled stream-of-consciousness burble where you spout a collection of words and hope they resonate with someone. It's not an elevator speech or a mission statement that sounds like everyone else. It is a methodical approach that differentiates you and invites someone to engage in a conversation. Keep in mind, you aren't trying to impress someone, you are trying to impress *upon* them what your points of difference are so that it *engages* them. I will talk about how to converge and integrate this with every form of communication you use, but for now let's put a framework together.

There are four cornerstones to creating a value proposition:

1. **Define your ideal client.**
2. **Define what your ideal client wants to achieve.**
3. **Define how you enable your clients to achieve their goals.**
4. **Define your process.**

These four definitions provide a foundation useful in many applications, including how to respond when you are asked the question "what do you do?"

Using this process, rather than tell someone what you do or what business you are in, connect it immediately with a quick description of who your ideal client is.

Who *is* your ideal client? If, from this moment forward, you predictably and consistently attracted only one type of client into your business, who would it be? Defining your ideal client is an important prerequisite to formalizing your branding.

1: Define your Ideal Client

Have you ever told your current clients, prospective clients and strategic partners who your ideal client is?

Don't keep it a mystery. This is an important step in improving the quality and quantity of referrals you receive.

I know a professional advisor who, during a gap analysis consultation, told me that in the previous 12 months he received eight referrals, but only one of those introductions perfectly resembled his ideal client profile. Twelve months later, after refining his approach, he received 16 referrals, 14 of which met his ideal client profile. He didn't become a better professional advisor in that window of time. He became better at articulating his value. He was always refer-able, but now his refer-ability is leading to a higher quality and quantity of introductions.

There are two key parameters I will remind you of here. First, stay true to the stewardship over salesmanship philosophy. In other words, don't talk about who you are *looking for* in terms of new clients. Instead, talk in terms of who you are *suited for*. It's all about who is a good fit; an alignment based on the needs of a client and how those needs align with your expertise.

It's attractive to convey to the world that you are a specialist and not a generalist.

When you get this right, you create an aspirational environment that naturally sifts good prospects from the mass of suspects. You're saying, "I'm not all things to all people, I'm all things to some people."

Let's say your ideal client is a successful business owner or professional. In that situation, the tip of the spear of your value proposition would be to say: *I'm a wealth advisor for a select group of very successful business owners and professionals.* If you don't want to paint yourself into a corner, add the word primarily. *I'm a wealth advisor, primarily for a small group of very successful business owners and professionals.* Or, *I'm a wealth advisor, primarily for a small group of successful individuals who are five years out or less from retirement,* or whatever the case may be.

The second thing I want to remind you of is to stick with a process. This time-tested approach is rooted in permission marketing. The core of permission marketing is to say something compelling to someone, prompting them to ask you a question for elaboration. Their question gives you *permission* to go into more detail. Rather than talking to a spectator, you are instead having a meaningful exchange with an engaged audience.

Five Irons, Fish Tanks and Yahtzee

Let me take this to some everyday examples.

As a professional advisor, it is tempting to try to impress a client or prospective client. The real skill, however, is impressing *upon* them that you are superior to any other alternative, and to have them come to that realization on their own.

Salespeople motivate people to take action. Consultants instill self-motivation and let people sell themselves.

As a parent, this hit home for me not long ago. I found myself over-leading and micromanaging my kids in a few areas and pushing them away as a result.

I would constantly tell one which golf club to use on a particular shot. I would take over the cleaning of the fish-tank and say "let me show you how it's done." I would even make suggestions as to what boxes to check after rolling dice in Yahtzee™.

Then it occurred to me: Let them fail in small tasks and figure it out for themselves.

It's tough as a dad, because you want to have all the answers and be the hero, but in preparing to let them go and face the world on their own, the safety net of micromanagement can become a hammock. Now, I strive to let them select the club and then offer insight and an assessment after the shot.

This is much easier to talk about than it is to put in practice, but it is worth the effort.

It may seem like a stretch to associate parenting to professional relationship management, but the nature of the communication in both situations is rooted in self-motivation and permission marketing. I've found conversations with my children blossomed when I avoided lecturing and data-dumping and instead asked questions and drove my commentary with brevity.

Whether it's heading up the lift at the ski hill, soaking in the tub *après-ski* or on one of many treks to an out-of-town sporting tournament, I see the power of engagement and human nature in action. Everyone likes to be heard and everyone likes to share their opinions, if we'll just create the right environment.

I was heading to a hockey tournament with one of my kids and, about midway in the trip, he asked me a great question: "What are your favorite books, Dad?"

I told him I had many favorites, but the top three would have to be *Les Miserables*, *The Count of Monte Cristo* and *Atlas Shrugged*. He responded by saying that he was familiar with the first two but completely unaware of the third.

"What is Atlas Shrugged about?" He asked.

I thought about it for a second. How do I possibly explain a 1200-plus-page novel printed in microscopic type, and do it briefly so that I don't bore him to tears droning on and ultimately push away his interest?

"It's a neat story about three types of people, the builders, the freeloaders and the destroyers," I said.

That was it. I left him wanting more and waited for him to give me permission to elaborate by asking me a follow-up question - and he did. It became a very memorable exchange for me.

Tighten up your message and be sequential in your delivery. With the intensity of noise and information, many people have the attention span of a hummingbird. Get to the point and leave them wanting more. Let them tell you how much information they need.

You can attract more ideal clients by making yourself attractive than all the hunter-gatherers out there with an "I eat what I kill" mentality can ambush.

The *Law of Resonance* is important to consider, here. It reminds us that the value of a good conversation begins when the talking stops. What resonates in a potential ideal client's mind when they walk out the door? An hour later? A day later? A week later? What became etched in their memory? What went to their head to die?

When you are defining a client, I'd like you to consider creating a panoramic and all-encompassing ideal client profile as part of the exercise. In keeping with professionalizing all aspects of your business down to the smallest detail, it is very helpful to get your ideal client out of your head and *fully defined* on paper. Once you do, you'll find many opportunities to use this in interactions in the future.

To ask it again, if you were to predictably and consistently only attract this one type of client into your business, who would it be? Frame this dream client using a structure that not only gives *you* clarity but also makes it clear for those who can be rainmakers for you.

For many years I've advised my clients to use a panoramic Triple-A Ideal Client Profile to define and describe their ideal client. Take a blank sheet of paper and jot down three 'A's along the left side from top to bottom. Start by filling in the various parameters and qualities that make up your ideal client.

The first A speaks to **Assets** – what are the specific needs and actions taken by an ideal client over the lifetime of your relationship with them? Don't use jargon like "affluent" or "high net worth". Be specific about their demographic, socioeconomic and other realities that speak to the alignment between their needs and your skills.

From there, shift to outlining the various **Attitudinal** qualities of your ideal client. You never dread seeing an ideal client's phone number on your call display, or an appointment with them on your calendar. Why is that? It's because they are in sync with you, they value you and they bring more to the table than just business.

The *Law of Environment* says that we are all products of our environment. If we associate with people who are negative and cynical, over time we will become products of that. It's subtle and gradual but it is infectious.

With that in mind, list eight or ten qualities of your ideal client. We'll take a deeper dive on this later in the book under the topic of client classification, but for now this is about reaching clarity yourself and then communicating that clarity to someone else so that they ultimately introduce the right people to you.

Quality introductions are by design, not by chance. Don't leave your rainmakers to their own devices trying to figure out who to introduce to you; tell them. In fact, many of our clients go so far as to show them. When they are in an engaged conversation with someone on the topic of who is a good fit, as an extension of their value proposition, they show a list of the qualities of their ideal clients. Things like:

They're nice people

They're engaged in my process without micromanaging

They're enlightened about the realities of market volatility

They focus on what I'm worth rather than what I cost

They're respectful of my team

They're responsible and resilient

They have gratitude for today and ambition for tomorrow

They're hard-working business owners or professionals

They're positive, optimistic and realistic

They have a strong sense of purpose

Having yourself and your team on the same wavelength about who your ideal client is can be powerful. It reflects well on you to be able to convey this to someone else in a structured format when the opportunity presents itself.

We'll go into more detail on this later, including defining knock-out factors and whether you'll need to disassociate from existing clients who don't meet your profile. For now, though, let's keep the context of this around defining your value proposition, which, incidentally, brings me the third A in the Triple-A Ideal Client Profile: ***Advocacy.***

Advocacy Comes by Design

The ideal client isn't just a client. They are an advocate. What does "advocate" mean to you? Many people, when asked to provide a definition for advocacy, say that "they are people who look out for me. They wave my flag. They're cheerleaders."

If that's what you're thinking, you're half right.

Who are they an advocate for? An advocate doesn't refer someone to you because they're trying to help you grow your business; they actually feel they are doing a friend a disservice by *not* making the introduction.

They're an advocate for both you *and the person they are introducing.*

You have a few people like this in your inner circle of relationships already, and the power of articulating your value and creating a fully integrated and converged branding strategy is that you can methodically create far more advocates.

This is by design.

To recap this, when you have the opportunity to describe what you do, the first thing I want you to convey is who your ideal client is, and then elaborate on that with Triple-A if someone invites you to expand on this positioning.

2: Define What They Want

Next, you want to speak to a specific hook that grabs someone's attention. Again, it's not what you say but rather what they hear that matters.

Over the years, there have been many branding strategies that demonstrate the power of the hook in terms of prompting a prospective client to think *"I get that! I want that."* In all forms of communication, a prospective client is interpreting your messaging within their inner dialogue and sifting through the noise to determine if the signal resonates.

Of all the examples I've seen, my favorite comes from Apple.

As of this writing, Apple is the most valuable company on the planet. It wasn't that long ago that Steve Jobs had to borrow $150 million dollars from Bill Gates. Apple was circling the drain and Jobs needed the capital to prompt the phoenix to rise from the ashes.

The product that led the renaissance was, of course, the iPod. The iPod was replacing CD players and was competing with MP3 players and services like Napster. Competitors, incidentally, who have either vanished or have been marginalized today by Apple's dominance of the market.

My point is this: Do you recall the branding strategy Apple used to launch the iPod? It was not a jargon-filled data-dump about how great their solution was. It was a simple hook: "One thousand songs in your pocket."

It's to the point. People quickly came to their own conclusions. *"I get that. I want that!"* The rest has been game-changing, highly disruptive and remarkable history.

The point is that your hook has to speak more to what your clients *want* rather than what it is you *do*. I see examples of this everywhere I go.

It wasn't long ago I went golfing with my son. It was a hot summer day and after the round we got into the car to head home. Immediately I said to him, "Buddy, roll down the window. It's time you took this hygiene thing seriously. You're getting older and your body is changing. Let's do a detour and go to the store to get you set up." I'm sure he rolled his eyes and said to himself, "Whatever!"

When we got to the store, I directed him to the massive wall containing every imaginable brand of shower gel, shampoo and body spray. Instantly, as if he were a zombie in a trance, he walked directly to one product – Axe™.

That's all he saw. Nothing else registered. I started laughing because I'm thinking to myself, "I just want my kid to be clean." He could care less about getting clean. That isn't what he wanted.

What did he want? He wanted to be just slightly more relevant to girls and he was convinced that Axe was going to get him there.

I soon realized that it doesn't even smell better than anything else (to me, at least) - and it didn't matter. For the first few days, the cloud of body spray around him made my eyes water, and it didn't matter. He came to his own conclusion as to what he wanted and he took action.

What is it that your ideal client wants?

Don't get into a data-dump about asset allocation, re-balancing and diversification, because you sound like everybody else and you're swimming in a pool of commoditized sameness. Speak to what the person *wants*.

If you work with business owners and professionals, do you know what they want? They want a work-optional lifestyle. They want to go to work because they want to, not because they have to. They aspire to financial independence. They want to be able to live off the income of their own resources.

With that addition, your value proposition begins to take shape: *"I'm a wealth advisor primarily for a select group of successful business owners and professionals who, among other things, aspire to a work-optional lifestyle."*

Stop there. Leave them wanting more. Let them process what you've said and then watch as they ask you questions that give you permission to elaborate to a far more engaged audience.

F.O.R.M.ing your Hook

A good exercise to help craft your unique hook, one that will speak to your ideal client, is driven by the F.O.R.M. process.

If you think about a twenty-minute conversation with a great client, you talk about their Family, Occupation, Recreation and Money. The first three relate to *why* financial independence is important to your clients. The last item speaks to *how* you get them there.

The more you talk about the why, the more value they will place in the how and, in the process, you differentiate and de-commoditize yourself and become indispensable to them.

If you have clients who are first-generation self-made affluent achievers, what do they want? They want to secure their family investment legacy. If you have clients approaching retirement, what do they want? They want to face the future with anticipation rather than apprehension, knowing that they won't outlive their money. They want to sleep well at night knowing that they can start checking off boxes on their bucket list.

Use this language and make it about their aspirations. They have goals and they are trying to determine if you are the means to those ends.

Talk about what clients value and they will place a higher value on your solutions. People are led, not pushed, and once they make that connection, you elevate how you are perceived.

3: Define How You Enable Your Clients to Achieve Their Goals

At this point you can connect what clients want with how you can get them there. That brings us to the third component in this process.

After you've defined your ideal client and used a hook to describe what those clients aspire to, explain *clearly* how you will bridge their goals to these outcomes and enable them to achieve their aspirations.

The truth is, clients often don't understand what you do.

You know what you do, but you're not marketing to yourself. Many of your clients don't fully understand *what* you do, let alone *all* that you do. You have to demystify it for them. This is where leadership and perpetual lifetime empowerment comes from.

Think about it this way: When you're at home and the power goes out, you call an electrician. He shows up. What do you want? You want the lights back on. Do you want to know everything he knows? Do you follow him around and ask him for the schematics of the breaker box? Perhaps you do, but I don't. I don't know how electricity works, and it doesn't matter. I know one thing; the electrician can fix it so that when I hit the switch the lights turn on, and that's about all I want to know.

Be the electrician for your clients. Be the switch, too. Say something that is so intuitive, so compelling, such a "*me-too*" that they just *get it*. Instead of saying "I help people", say this, "*I have developed and refined a process that puts all the pieces of the financial puzzle together for my clients.*"

What will a prospective client hear when you say that? It conveys experience and mileage. Do you want your clients to talk about you, the person, or do you want the clients to talk about you, the person, *and* your process? It's not just the messenger, it's the message, as well. You want them to buy into all this. Define it. Here is what they'll hear; "*I've developed and refined a process that puts all the pieces of the puzzle together for people who want what YOU want*", and you know what that prospective client is going to say to you.

In their inside voice they are going to say, *I get that. I want that, because I don't have that right now. I just have a guy that keeps trying to sell me stuff.* "I want a process, how does that work?" they'll think, and probably ask outright.

They're giving you permission to go into more detail. This is why yo. don't data-dump, don't initially go into more detail and leave them wanting more until they give you permission. Now, they're engaged. When someone asks how your process works, you can initially talk in symbolic terms and metaphors. You can ask: *"Have you ever tried to solve a jigsaw puzzle without the picture from the box lid?"*

They'll probably agree that is the hard way to do it. They just gave you permission to elaborate on your process.

The other benefit of this approach is that you can future-pace the relationship. This ensures that your clients don't focus solely on what you have provided to them up to now. Instead, they start to understand the dynamic and fluid nature of their needs over the long term. Rather than buying products and solutions, they are buying into your process. This ensures that, as their life unfolds and their needs evolve, they know you will put all the pieces of the puzzle together to guarantee they have the complete picture.

That is the epitome of empowerment. It's not about wallet share or selling your clients on new services, it's about a process that is positioned as a benefit to the client for the lifetime of the relationship.

Let's get back to our process. Tell the prospect who your ideal client is and tell them what they want. Tell them how you get them there. Tell them you've developed and refined a process.

Finally, call your process something.

4: Define your Process - Give It a Name

Take the abstract nature of what you do and make it intuitive and compelling. Give it some personality, identity and make it real. Call it something.

It's a handle the prospective client can grab onto. It keeps a client locked into you and can also competitor-proof them. It will not only capture money in motion as life unfolds, but also prompts them to be more than a client; to be a referral-generating advocate because you made it so easy to wave the flag. They can communicate this to somebody else and they will get it, too.

Let me give you another real-world example.

My family decided to go camping. We needed a new tent. When you set out to buy something new you make a mental checklist of what you *want*. What do you want in a tent? When you want a new tent you want many things, but what do you really want? What's at the top of the list?

t to be dry. Sure, I want it to be easy to maintain and well made. I assemble quickly and fold up easily and fit back into the bag, etc., top of the list, I want to be dry.

Of the tents I looked at, one tent mentioned on the features and benefits sheet that it had a fly. The fact-sheet told me all the reasons why the fly was a good thing.

Ultimately, a fly is a commodity.

Another tent had the WeatherTek ™ system. That sounded official. It sounded like some research went into that. You know what the WeatherTek system is? It's a fly. Which one sounded better? This tent has a fly. That tent has the WeatherTek system.

Which tent did I buy? You can guess. Is the WeatherTek system better than a fly? It doesn't matter, because the choice was made on which one resonated with me.

Call your process something. Give it a name. Being "better" doesn't matter. It's not what it *is*, it's what I *think* it is. Make it proprietary. Trademark it and integrate it within all aspects of your branding strategy, because full convergence of your messaging gives you sustained traction and reinforces value.

Here's a complete example: *"I'm a wealth advisor primarily for a select group of very successful business owners and professionals, who among other things aspire to a work-optional lifestyle. I've developed and refined a process to put all the pieces of that puzzle together and I call it the D3 investment process. D3 stands for Discovery, Design and Deploy."*

Does that sound better than "I help people achieve their financial goals?"

Does it make me a better professional advisor today than I was before I evolved my value proposition? Again, you're not marketing to yourself. You're not trying to impress people, you're trying to impress *upon* them that you're superior, that you can be trusted and are an attractive option.

The perception people have of you will be impacted by your branding. You're defining yourself as an upgrade to their current advisor.

Think about an airline flight – when you look at coach versus first class, and you're upgraded to first – how do you feel? That's how a client or prospective client will feel about what you are defining for them.

I don't mean to over-simplify this, but I do this all the time. I don't know how many names I've come up with for professional advisors that want to brand what they do. When you call it something it becomes the *Intel inside* sticker on your computer. On the bottom of your e-mails it says "ask me about the D3 investment process". On your website and LinkedIn it says "Home of the D3 investment process".

Whatever you call it, just have the structure and get into the habit of imprinting and embedding it on everything you do.

Your named process becomes your Nike Swoosh. You don't even have to explain it anymore, people will just *get it*. If somebody asks, "How does this work?" they are giving you permission to go into more detail. This is what provides that persuasive impact.

If I'm your client, you don't want me saying to a friend, "you have to talk to my advisor, I really trust her." That trust is a given. You want me to say, "I really like my advisor, I really trust her, but more importantly than that, I've had other advisors in the past, and I've never felt more comfortable about the track I'm on because of her process."

That is where persuasive impact is born. If I'm your client, I can be much more compelling to a friend than you'll ever be. Because of their alignment with you and with your process, they understand your value and they can articulate it clearly to somebody else.

How long does all this take? The advisors I've worked with over the years have to be taken on an individual basis. Sometimes I crack the code in 45 minutes. With others it takes 45 days. It's not an exact science. There is no time frame here. It is, however, very common that when we do crack the code the advisor says to me, "I love this, it's fantastic. I can get behind this, but now I have to come up with a process." I laugh and tell them they already have a process. They just don't refer to it as one, and therefore people don't understand and appreciate what they do.

So start calling it a process.

Adding the word Method, System, Process, Solution, Approach or Formula to the end of what you call your process makes it more tangible and puts it well on its way to becoming proprietary. Not only trademarking it, but also securing the appropriate website domain can enable you to amplify its value.

We've seen The Cascade FORMula that speaks to the importance of cash-flow and proactive planning. The SWAN Process that speaks to the enabling clients to Sleep Well At Night. The Beacon 360 Method that supports the premise of navigation and a holistic, panoramic solution. The Bridging Approach that defines you as the bridge to your clients' goals.

Many professional advisors talk about Family Investment Legacy Planning. Fewer use a tree as a symbol to make that process concrete and immediately understandable. Using a name and a symbol gives your process personality and allows you to explain it clearly to your clients. That fully converged and integrated imprint makes it safe and compelling for someone to transmit that message and introduce you up, down and throughout their family.

Subtle things like wall décor, greeting cards and other collateral can help tie it all together. Using imagery like this is something I will go into more detail on in the *Multi-sensory Office* section.

If you're going tell the world you have a process it does help to actually have a process. I don't know your situation; I don't know where I caught you in your business, but there are various ways to demonstrate you *do* have a process.

The resources I will provide in this book will help you drill down and make your own process complete and concrete.

How Are You Described?

The way you articulate your value goes beyond how you are perceived. It also impacts how you are *described*.

If I'm your client and a friend gives me the opportunity to shine a light on you, what do I say? If a strategic partner is asked by a client to endorse someone in your field, what does he or she say? How do they describe you?

I ask this question whenever I conduct a gap analysis: *How do your clients describe you?*

Most professional advisors say they have no idea. Here is a vital piece of actionable advice: Make your clients the voice you listen to. I'll say it again and again throughout this book: *Listen to your clients.* They are on the receiving end of your value and your service. Who better to articulate that value to somebody else?

When a client does describe you to someone, do they talk about you in generalities, pleasantries and platitudes? It's not negative if a client tells a friend that they "really like and trust you" because you "take good care of them". But they're really endorsing the person, not your process – the messenger rather than your message.

Wouldn't it be great if your clients really knew how to describe you and your process in a compelling and persuasive way?

One of the best ways to get a sense for where you're at in the eyes of your clients is to contact them on the phone and ask them this:

"As you know, we take service very seriously but we never want to get complacent. We always want to find ways to raise the bar when it comes to the client experience and the best way to do that is to ask the people on the receiving end. So, if you don't mind me asking, what's the one thing you value most about our relationship?"

Their response will be close to how they describe you to a friend or family member. If you want to go a little deeper, the next time you get a referral from a client or partner, call them up and thank them for the endorsement. And then ask:

"When I met your friend I have to say he was so predisposed and engaged in the conversation that I'm curious as to what you said. How did you describe me?"

If you are going to ask this, brace yourself. You're probably not going to like what they say. Not because it's negative, but because they're talking about you in generalities. They'll say, "I really trust you, I like you, you're with a great firm."

That does not stand out. That is not compelling. If your clients can't describe you to *you*, they certainly can't describe you to someone else.

Don't stop at clients and partners. As part of your research, ask your staff to describe you. It's not uncommon for a team of five people to give five different descriptions.

Going forward, you can take the steps to ensure that everyone is consistently representing your value and you're not swimming in a pool of generic sameness.

The power of this concept – and the need for it - was revealed to me over the years while conducting countless gap analyses. The importance of that one simple question, "how are you described", was undeniable.

I don't know how many times I've asked the question, but I can tell you the number of people who could describe themselves with clarity was a much smaller number.

The Battle of the Bland

I asked a substantial professional advisor in California with 21 years of experience how his clients described him.

"Man I hate that question," he said.

"You've only had 21 years to answer it, so I can see how I caught you off guard," I said.

"I know what you're saying. Are you asking me for my elevator speech or pitch book or my mission statement?"

"Stop right there," I said. "Look, everything you say and everything you communicate to a client is either a 'me-too' or a 'so-what.'"

A 'me-too' speaks directly to a client and amplifies how you are described, which attracts that person and engages them. In their inside voice they say to themselves *"I want that."* Or, it's a *so-what*. A so-what they dismiss. It's the same as everybody else. It's just noise. You sound like Charlie Brown's teacher.

I want you to think about this. It's not a mission statement. It's not a pitch book. That's what salespeople use. Consultants use a value proposition, a verbal extension of their branding strategy that's integrated and converged.

After my rant, the advisor told me, "I'm a professional advisor and I help people reach their financial goals."

I said that is completely accurate, but you just described about 10,000 professional advisors.

You can't bore someone into buying something. It sounds like everybody else, and it's too easy to dismiss. Plus, what does it even mean? It's abstract, without specifics people can grasp.

What does it mean when you say "I help people?" You need to think about that answer as it applies to you and your business.

Let's Shoot Your Trailer

As you near the end of this first section, I have a question: Have you created a trailer of your overall philosophy, planning strategy and process?

Hollywood promotes a movie using a brief trailer to get your attention, whet your appetite and leave you wanting more. What do you say in the three or four minutes at the beginning of a meeting with a prospective client to define your value to them?

The following is an exercise that will help focus your prospective clients. It will concisely tell them why they want to work with you as you're having your initial meeting. It will make you unforgettable and indispensable.

It starts with a basic Venn diagram. In your meeting, turn your agenda over and draw two circles about the size of hockey pucks that just intersect. Label the left one "Matters" and the right "Control".

You can introduce the graphic by explaining why you're doing it. For example, *"The beauty of our process is that it ensures we never lose sight of two essential elements to achieving financial independence."*

These two elements are what *matters* and what you can *control*.

Start with what matters to your client. Vertically, jot down the following letters below the "matters" circle: F, O, R and M. Walk the client through each.

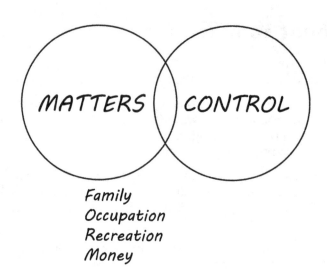

Family
Occupation
Recreation
Money

F is family – The number-one concern to your client – the thing that matters most. You can touch on concepts like the family investment legacy, but the basic truth is that clients want to work with you if they know you understand that their family matters. Punctuate it by saying *"We never lose sight of that."*

O is occupation – The client may aspire to a work-optional lifestyle or they may want to retire completely and be confident of their ability to do so without outliving their money, but whatever their focus, their occupation, past or future, is on their mind. Again, punctuate it by saying *"We never lose sight of that."*

R is recreation – We all have a bucket list, things we want to do, places we want to see, and having the time and security to do them is something we all understand. We want to face the future with anticipation. And again: *"We never lose sight of that."*

Connect those three with a bracket and jot down "WHY" beside them. You've just defined why your client wants a professional with a stewardship mindset to work with them.

For M – Write "money" and, beside it, write "HOW". Money is how you accomplish the previous three vital matters. I'll say it again: The more emphasis you place on *why* financial independence is important to your client, the more value they will place on *how* you get them there and, in the process, you differentiate yourself, become indispensable and de-commoditize your value.

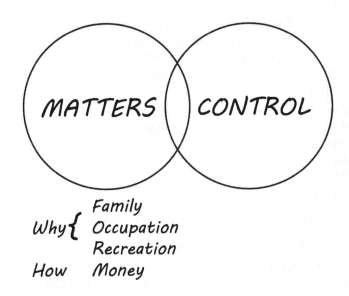

Now jump to the right-hand "Control" circle.

You can say something like the following: *"In life, there are many things that are out of our control and, frankly, I don't spend a lot of time worrying about them. Instead, I focus on the set of your sail rather than the direction of the wind."* Jot down three vertical "Ps" and fill each out in order.

The first is **Philosophy**. Express your understanding of the importance of panoramic wealth and risk management, of dealing with the puzzle that is the intersection of your client's needs and the forces around him, your role in stewardship and not salesmanship – these are your points when discussing your philosophy.

The second P is **Planning**. You have a strategy. You don't jam square pegs in round holes – you craft a strategy that addresses the client's needs and brings clarity to their situation – more on this, shortly. You implement all this through the third P: **Process**. Everything you do is driven by a process, set to sync with the client's future pace as their life and needs unfold – and that process, in turn, is driven by three Ds:

Step One - **Discovery**: Which gives us *clarity*.

Step Two - **Design**: Which gives us *comfort*.

Step Three - **Deploy**: Which gives us *confidence* that all the pieces of the puzzle are in place, clearly understood and focused to address the needs of the client, driven by what matters - their *why*. This gives us a complete picture.

That overlap in the middle? That's where you can best serve their needs. That's the point of "fit" – that's the part where your service as a steward matters – so take your pen and color that section in for your client. Tell them *"that's where we live."*

If you want, sweep your pen over that sideways "8" repeatedly to make an infinity symbol and say *"that's why I have second and third generation clients."*

Be a broken record as you work through the diagram– *"this is a step in our process – we have developed and refined in our process – there is a process in place..."*

It's not what you say, it's what they hear within their frame of reference. With the way you've cast yourself in this "trailer", you make sure that other messages don't stand up in comparison. Others sound like they have one year of experience 18 times while you sound like you have invested the past into the future and have cracked the code.

Don't use jargon. Don't bore them with the technical and the detailed about "how" you do your job. Jargon is endemic to every industry, and if you use it you will be lost in the crowd. This approach elevates you from the pack. Be clear, brief and direct. Let the client reveal to you how much more detail they need on your process. Some people want to know how to build a watch, others just want to know the time.

What will also differentiate and elevate you in the client's eyes is if you *listen*. Listen to the client's concerns and desires and understand their "why". Learn what is important, and use that when talking to other clients. You'll show them you are a professional with a process that values communication.

Listen to learn, not to buy time to think about your reply.

Tie your trailer in with your symbol and your unique value proposition to give it personality. Facts tell, stories sell.

Most importantly, this approach resonates immediately and it stays etched in their minds when they walk out the door. It's when they aren't in front of you – while they are driving home from the meeting - that the value of this impacts a relationship and makes you stand head and shoulders above the rest.

Planning is Panoramic

Planning, philosophy and process are all interdependent. Educating a prospective client as to why this is – or re-framing your value with an existing client through the three Ps – helps them buy into your positioning as a professional consultant.

We've touched on Philosophy and Process, but let me expand on Planning.

Planning is a four-fold, panoramic process. In addition to not being a square-peg/round-hole template as you reassured your prospective client in your trailer, there are four central pillars you need clarity on, and that you must communicate to the client.

A planning process for a client encompasses Wealth Management, Risk Management, Tax Management and Debt Management. It bridges your philosophy to your strategy.

A *Wealth management* process focuses on diversification. It follows the path of selling on rallies and buying on retreats and binds clients to your process rather than the emotional upheavals of the market.

Risk management is just that. As the industry rises and falls, you, as an income producer, make or protect money for your clients no matter the smoothness of the road or the sudden appearance of potholes. If you had a machine that printed money, you'd insure it, knowing that to have insurance and not need it is preferable to needing it and not having it. The market is the machine – your services are the insurance.

Tax management is always a concern for any client. It's incumbent on the taxpayer to be savvy, not the tax man. That's why tax management is such a vital function. The tax man will do it for you – but he'll also take every penny he can get. What's the difference between tax evasion and tax avoidance? About seven years, according to the old joke. Tax management makes sure that remains a joke instead of a sentence.

Debt management is being positioned for anything, at any time. Critical life events will occur, for everyone, and good decisions always stem from strong positions.

Again, the important thing here is not that you, the professional advisor, know all four quadrants of your planning process, how your philosophy infuses them all and how your process delivers them – that's assumed – it's that you educate your client or potential client so they know, as well.

Hands-On in a Hands-Free World

Now that we've charted the path to crafting your unique value proposition, philosophy and process, let me talk about the concept of vapor to paper – of getting it out of your head and making it real.

First of all, think about how much technology has crept into our lives. Think about the corollary to that: The higher the velocity of technological change, the more the human touch matters.

Is there anything about what you do and provide as part of your service model that a client or prospective client can hold in their hands? Something that is not a product brochure, a performance statement or a policy?

All of that is the message. I'm talking about something that reminds a client of you, the messenger.

Here's a simple and effective example: What if you were to send a Thanksgiving card to your best clients this year? A lot of people send a holiday card in December. It goes on the mantle next to the ones from their vet, their mechanic and their chiropractor. A Thanksgiving card is unique. The client can hold it in their hands and you can say thanks for a great relationship. It's powerful. It arrives on its own, it stands out and it shows you thought of them.

Don't just go through the motions. People sort their mail over a garbage can. If your cards are boring, then just throw them in your own trash and save yourself the stamps.

The goal is to own the mantle. If you send a card, it stays on the mantle; it has impact and shelf life. It stops them in their tracks and they can't bear to throw it away. The ROI on these cards is immense because it's not vapor. It doesn't go to their heads to die.

Another example - a client calls you up and says, "You have got to talk to my friend, he just inherited some money and sold his business and he's a little freaked out. Can you talk to him?"

After you contact that friend, send an introductory kit to him by two-day courier. Something he can hold in his hands to help him develop a relationship with you before he meets you. It builds anticipation for the meeting, builds contrast between you and his current advisor and validates the value of meeting you.

Don't stop there. Do you use an agenda when you meet with a prospective client or existing client? We'll delve deeply into this later in the book, but initially it's important to note that you must always have an agenda, simple or not, when meeting a client or a prospect. An agenda is a track to follow and it's another physical thing a client can hold.

When you onboard a client, do you provide them with a beautiful binder to welcome them? An impressive binder they can hold? Some people might say, "I used to do that a long time ago and it worked, but I stopped doing it as everything became more virtual."

Binders may sound a little horse and buggy, but, as I said before, the more technology creeps into our lives, the more the human touch matters. Your website, emails and the rest support the message, but the binder and the human touch support the messenger.

Most people stop providing physical interactions like these because they think that technology can replace the binder or the card. The truth is just the opposite. The binder is more relevant now than in the old days. It's a trophy that can be touched.

When you show a prospective client that binder, tell them, *"I take great pride in helping my clients stay clear on the track they are on. The dashboards and website and log-ons are all great, but this is the hub".* Say to the client, *"There are so many things that I provide to my clients, some of which are not relevant to you today, but as your life unfolds and your needs evolve my job is to get out in front of that and put the pieces together."*

In the binder, you show them your full array of services.

Not only does this binder competitor-proof and insulate them, it captures money in motion and uncovers hidden assets. It is also the tangible springboard to advocacy.

The binder process is also exceptional when it comes to re-framing your relationships with existing clients.

The *Law of Familiarity* suggests that relationships drift into a pattern over time in which things can be taken for granted and your value trivialized. You can breathe new life into an old relationship with a re-framing process anchored by the binder.

Clients are under constant siege from the noise of the media and your competitors. If your service model provides 30 touches in a year for a Triple-A client, then there are still 335 days where the client is left alone with their thoughts.

The binder is the glue that's there every day.

Do You Need to Become a Better Advisor to Get Better Results?

Short answer? No.

Your branding is like staging a house. Think of a fundamentally sound home with a terrific location, solid construction and excellent design. It is valued at a million dollars. Then a design expert comes along and throws $20,000 of tasteful staging at the home and it sells for 1.3 million.

Is it, measurably, any more valuable? Of course not, and the professional advisor who doubles their business through an impeccable client experience and well-structured branding and value proposition is using the same strategy. They aren't any better at their core solutions. The perception of value is enhanced, though. Like the staged home, the professional is appreciated more than before.

All this speaks directly to *The Law of Resonance*. The true value of your communication begins when the conversation is over. Ask yourself: What is resonating as they walk out the door? Some things are more memorable than others. Some things are etched into the person's memory while others don't make it to the parking lot. If you just talk, the value will be temporary. If you structure your words in a way that checks off the question boxes in the person's mind *before they were actively thinking about them*, your persuasive impact will be far greater.

Framing your ideal client with AAA and actually writing that on their agenda for them to see has greater resonance than only talking about your ideal client.

Your words have much more persuasive impact when they are structured. It reminds me of the book *Every Shot Must Have a Purpose* written by golf instructors Pia Nilsson and Lynn Marriott. They contend that every shot must be prefaced by a pre-shot routine and structure. It's the same with your words – they need structure to be more purposeful. You must not merely *talk* but *communicate*. This is how you differentiate and become one in a million rather than one of a million.

It also reminds me of an advisor who works with Gen X and Y clients with substantial assets and sophisticated and perpetually evolving needs. He used to data-dump a prospective client trying to impress him or her. Instead, I suggested that he impress upon the prospective client that he was superior to their soon-to-be-former advisor.

Now, he asks a lot of questions, engages the prospective clients, maintains brevity and elevates the conversation so that the prospective client achieves validation, contrast and self-motivation.

He starts by asking this: *"Let me quickly provide you a high-level overview of my philosophy, planning strategy and process. Before I do, though, can I ask; did you ever play Tetris as a kid?"* (Considering his target market, virtually everyone says "yes" – if not, he explains the premise of the game.)

He then says: *"I think of that as a metaphor for my client's life: Increasing velocity over time with a goal of putting all the blocks in place in an orderly manner."*

He then asks: *"Are you where you said you were going to be five years ago?"* Most people say in some ways yes and in other ways no.

He follows with: *"Can you believe it's already almost (whatever year it's about to be)? Did the last five years seem like a bit of a blur?"* Everyone nods affirmatively.

He then asks: *"Would you agree that the next five years will probably zip by even faster – a blink of an eye?"* Again, there is lots of nodding.

He then says: *"I'm asking all of this because that's where I fit into my clients' lives. Like a Tetris player, I have a process that puts all the pieces of the financial puzzle together as life unfolds and needs evolve. We stay true to an enlightened philosophy centered on achieving financial independence and we use a personalized planning strategy that is designed to steer our clients towards a work-optional lifestyle. Along the way, ultimately we want to help our clients slow life down, restore liberation and order and ensure they are enjoying the fruits of their work ethic and sense of purpose. Does that make sense?"*

If the prospective client starts talking about short term performance or specific stocks or sectors, the advisor steps in and says, *"It's important for you to know my philosophy. Some advisors fixate on products, pricing and performance – that's not me. I believe the markets are like the seasons. When things are rocking along, we are in the autumn harvest. Now how often does winter follow autumn? Approximately, how often? Every time. When markets are rising, I think winter. When markets are volatile and dropping, I think spring. The most successful investors in the world, whose results are enduring, share this same philosophy. If you are thinking short term, I'm probably not the advisor for you."*

The premise with this approach is to use metaphors, symbols and intrigue to create an energy and personality to your value; to de-commoditize yourself.

Again, the Socratic approach with brevity as the driver is the key. You have to intervene with yourself when you start data-dumping. It's like the governor on a golf cart. Slow down, stay in control and you'll stay out of the rough. You'll fast-track new clients to advocate status and you'll effectively re-frame existing relationships so that they will understand and appreciate your value fully, thus enabling them to relay it more effectively to people they know.

First, *take action*. This quick-start section should have you moving forward with a road-map in place. Now you can proceed into a deeper dive on the tools that will help you rise to the next level and be among the best.

Visit **www.TheAdvisorPlaybook.com** for access
to the Playbook Implementation Program

Section 2: Strategic planning

Analyze your gaps

Plans are nothing, but planning is everything
- President Dwight Eisenhower

Controlling the Controllable

Market volatility, political uncertainty, competitive forces and various external dependencies are facts of life for a knowledge-for-profit professional.

It would be great if the world cooperated with our plans on a consistent basis, but that is not the way it is. Let's face it; that's why clients hire you. Friction and uncertainty come with the territory. Your ability to deal with this reality is a major factor that separates the best from the rest.

Strategic planning is the first step in focusing that ability. In many ways, strategic planning acts like the noise-canceling headphones I talked about earlier. As with your clients, there is a sea of noise competing for *your* attention, and the velocity and volume increases every year. A strategic planning process lets you tune out the static and improve the signal-to-noise ratio. This ensures that you focus on what matters - the things you have control over and that have real importance - so you can move in the direction of your vision for the future, relying less on hope and more on process. It gives you the guide you need to begin constructing something of greater value.

I'll come back to the jigsaw analogy: Have you ever tried to assemble a jigsaw puzzle without the picture as a reference to guide you? It can be done through trial and error, but it takes far longer and is far more frustrating without a frame of reference. A personalized strategic plan serves as your guide as you put the pieces of both life and business together.

A strategic plan can help you make critical observations about the track you are on, based on the *Law of Cause and Effect*, to ensure that you're engaged in the activities that contribute to your productivity goals. It can help you identify untapped opportunities and overlooked vulnerabilities, so you take action accordingly.

The key is to apply a process, and not go through that process in isolation.

My approach to strategic planning is driven in large part by the gap analysis I discussed. Rather than a generic pep-talk that tells someone what they should be doing and has temporary value, I use a Socratic approach, asking a series of questions that act as a strategic analysis and a path to discovery and self-motivation. I've had countless exchanges with professionals over the years where our process leads them to their own conclusions about what really matters and how to make it all a reality.

As an example, I was speaking with a professional advisor recently as part of a strategic planning conversation. We were deep into a conversation on business development, client acquisition and onboarding when we reached the following sequence of simple questions.

"Do your clients fully understand and appreciate your value?" I asked.

After a long pause, he replied with a tentative, "I think they do."

I then asked him, "How do your clients describe you?"

"I have no idea, really. They probably say they trust and believe in me," he said.

"What is your process to make your clients the voice you listen to in order to get the pulse on the effectiveness of your communications?" I asked.

To which he replied, "I don't have one."

It is common for professionals from all walks of life to drift into a pattern of sporadic client communication and assume that all is well - part of that inertia confidence I mentioned. While their approach isn't necessarily bad *per se*, it certainly isn't firing on all cylinders.

In the scenario I described, I brought the conversation to the tipping point a few questions later by asking about the advisor's approach to onboarding new clients. He proceeded to outline his method, which was fine, but which had several gaps. I then asked him why he did things the way he did, to which he replied, "That's basically the way we've always done it."

It is essential that you constantly scrutinize your procedures in order to optimize and refine how you do things. There is a place for the "if it ain't broke, don't fix it" mantra, but when it comes to communication - especially as it relates to competitor-proofing clients, gaining their full empowerment as the relationship unfolds, and new client acquisition through referrals - you can't take anything for granted.

You must continually strive to raise the bar, and to do that you need to know where you stand.

The advisor I just described is a classic example of someone with significant mileage and experience whose efforts compounded over time, but had brought him to a plateau. In many ways he was mistaking *movement* for *achievement*. He didn't need to repair any damage, and he definitely didn't need to make any drastic wholesale changes or reinvent the wheel. He simply needed to make some minor adjustments.

It's not an exact science but I've seen time and time again how very successful advisors have done 80 percent of the necessary work on their business, but are only realizing about 20 percent of the reward. A few simple refinements are all that were needed to unlock the full potential.

Crack the Code: Make it Actionable

Ultimately, a strategic plan is only helpful if the ideas identified can be translated into results.

You want your business legacy to reflect your commitment to helping people face the future with anticipation *and* to be an action-oriented implementer. Strategic planning isn't just about crystallizing your thoughts on paper. It's also about the application of appropriate strategies that will propel you forward.

Let's circle back to the three numbers in the combination that you need to dial-in to unlock your full potential:

- **Core Solutions Process** - The solutions you provide.

- **Practice Management** - Running your business like a business.

- **Relationship Management** – Articulating and communicating your value.

Most professional advisors I work with are solid on the core solutions side but have gaps in their practice and relationship management. As the knowledge-for-profit industries become more commoditized, the proprietary value and untapped potential is amplified in those areas. Contrast their value with your core solutions, which, no matter how excellently delivered, are not proprietary. They're not unique. Any other professional advisor can offer some or all of them.

When you lock in all three numbers, you create efficiency, consistency and increased profitability. It sounds trite, but it's about working smarter, not harder, and identifying where the veins of gold lie. A strategic planning process can help you locate them.

Of all the focal points I identify when conducting a gap analysis with a professional advisor, one of the most important is helping them fully understand what it is they get paid to do. Then, I help create a structure and environment so that's *all* that they do. Experience has shown that, with the benefits of laser focus and continual compounding, those activities will bring the advisor to their productivity goals.

Before you say you're too busy to worry about strategic planning; we're all busy. The question is: Busy doing what? As every month goes by, distractions attempt to lure you away from your focus. If you take the bait you run the risk of drifting away from your goals.

Stepping back, assessing your current approach and then creating a strategic plan is an often-overlooked but non-optional component allowing continual progress in business. To avoid sounding preachy, let me admit that this is easier to talk about than it is to do. Like the old expression about the cobbler's children having no shoes, as business consultants we often find ourselves assisting clients with their strategic plans and neglecting our own. Inevitably, it comes back to bite us. This neglect usually creeps in when we are swamped and "too busy" to plan for the future.

Busy isn't a synonym for productive. Strategic planning helps to minimize the miscues and maximize the opportunities.

The days are long but the years are short - Gretchen Rubin

If you are like most people I work with, five years ago you had a vision for where you would be today. Have you arrived at that place? How did you arrive where you are? Was it by design? Was it market lift? It's not uncommon, with all the forces pulling at you, to drift into a pattern without realizing it until you apply some hindsight.

Perhaps you said that you would start taking Fridays off. Maybe you said that you would transition to a fee-for-service model. Right-sizing might have been something you'd considered. Fair enough. Chances are that life is still pretty good, even if it hasn't played out exactly as you envisioned. Looking forward, though, you have to ask yourself, "What does my ideal life look like in the next five years and how am I going to get there?"

A long-time and extremely results-oriented coach of ours reminded me of this powerful quote during a conversation about strategic planning: "You don't really know someone until you've spent some time with them on paper." Having the focus to get everything out of your head and put it all on paper forces clarity of thought and encourages a deliberate attempt to quantify what is important. It serves as a blueprint to help you see past short-term obstacles while tuning out more of life's distortion and noise. As you embark on your business journey, your strategic plan acts as a GPS enabling you to make mid-course corrections early, before you are too far off-track.

Small deviations may not seem important at first, but the further off-track you become, the further you are from your goals and ideal life.

An *Ideal Life* Primer

Here are a few of the goals professionals have opened up to me about in relation to resetting their approach:

I want to restore liberation and order to my life. I'm tired of fire-fighting, micro-managing and babysitting.

You want to run the business so that it's not running you, but it has to be more than a goal. You have to apply a process that helps everyone on your team to get the business out of their heads and into a playbook. It's a process to turn your book into an actual business, rather than having just a book of business.

I don't want any dead branches in my business. It's time to prune the high-maintenance clients but I'm not sure where to start.

You've heard the expression that there are only so many seats on the plane and you have to respect that capacity? Right-sizing needs to be done and it needs to be done professionally and respectfully. It must to be based on mutual fit and, if done properly, you create capacity for more first-class passengers while ensuring an environment that affluent clients aspire to belong to.

I want to transition to a fee-for-service model but I'm nervous about how my clients will respond.

If clearly communicated as an upgrade, with tangible improvements to your client service model, your clients will focus on what you're worth rather than what you cost. Later in this book, I'll go into this particular transition in detail.

I want to stop trading my time for money and start building more equity value in my business.

When you de-personalize your business by going beyond raw talent and instead focus on your ongoing and progressive process, you can evolve from a production mindset to an asset mindset. Your business can be worth far more than it is today.

The gist of this is simple. A strategic planning process can reveal where adjustments and refinements can be made in your business. Few advisors I work with are way off track, or need dramatic wholesale changes to the way they conduct themselves.

Case in point, in our on-going practice management coaching with professional advisors, I often remind our clients of this simple fact: Being a great professional advisor, in and of itself, is no guarantee for success in this business. I have seen time and time again where the most effective advisors with limitless growth and progress potential aren't necessarily the most sophisticated asset managers.

The common thread, however, is that they are the most effective at practice and relationship management.

History provides countless examples of the need to possess strong business acumen along with vital core skills. One of my favorites is the rivalry between Nikola Tesla and Thomas Edison, two inventors who both made enormous contributions to society, but who had dramatically different outcomes in life. Edison's company became General Electric, while Tesla sold his patents to Westinghouse and died alone and in debt.

While you can argue that Tesla was a better inventor than Edison, Edison's business and branding skills were far superior.

I will never trivialize the importance of being a skilled professional in your core solutions, but it is a given that you are effective there. My point is this: There is little correlation between how professionally skillful you are and how successful you will ultimately be in terms of unlocking your full potential.

The days of building the better mouse trap and the world beating a path to your door are long gone. Ongoing professional development to sharpen your skills is essential, but do you invest the same amount of time sharpening your practice- and relationship-management processes? They are of equal importance.

Many professional advisors I work with are successful, enjoy an impressive lifestyle and should be content, but many of them are still ambitious and are frustrated because they have hit a plateau. While every advisor's scenario is unique, often the plateau stems from inertia confidence. Simply put, the advisor is busy repeating habits and patterns, and has been for an extended period of time. They are getting results, but they can raise the bar and achieve more.

Every advisor can drift into a rut when they haven't stepped outside of their business to kick their own tires and assess where they can make refinements to their approach. This is especially important if you want to continually increase the quality of clients you are attracting.

From Commodity to Communication

I had a conversation with an advisor who primarily has a Business to Business approach as opposed to a Business to Consumer model. This advisor provides group plans and related products to business owners and was spending a lot of time explaining his core solutions to prospective clients.

He spent very little time understanding the nuances of each business or explaining his service model and value proposition, however. As a result, he was swimming in the pool of sameness and had an average closing ratio. Worse than that, though, was that the quality and quantity of referrals he was attracting was brutal.

After analyzing his communications methodology, branding and service process, I provided some minor adjustments that he could deploy. Today, he spends far more time being interested in the prospective client's business, outlining his points of difference and setting expectations as they relate to ongoing service – all driven by process.

Business owners understand the importance of process and they can identify someone just trying to make a sale versus someone who is focused on the lifetime value of a client relationship. Furthermore, this client has started to re-frame his relationships with existing clients to ensure they understand and appreciate his current service model, and he's now outlining how he will enhance service provided going forward.

This not only serves as the foundation for a competitor-proofed relationship, but also gains a client's full empowerment and creates consistent advocacy.

Are You on the Verge?

I recently talked to an advisor who made a number of small refinements to his approach and the results have been staggering. Specifically, he shifted from an elevator speech that sounded like everyone else to a variation of our value proposition (following the four-point process outlined earlier) that is to the point and compelling.

He used to say, *"I help affluent clients manage their wealth and risk."* Today he says, *"I am a wealth advisor, primarily for successful business owners who aspire to a work-optional life-style. I've developed a process that manages wealth and risk for my clients."*

That small adjustment positions this advisor as a consultant with a process, so that he isn't perceived as just another broker with a generic approach.

After a small informal survey, he told me that his clients previously described him to friends as "a good guy with good ideas". Today they describe him as a professional with a process. That small distinction creates a much more favorable perception of relevant and unique value.

The Rookie with 15 Years of Experience

As each year winds down, you probably spend a fair amount of time on strategic planning, goal setting and trying to determine how to take your business to the next level.

Chances are that you ponder your business, assessing how close the results you achieved lined up with the goals and objectives you established the previous year. Did this year play out as you had hoped? Did you meet, exceed, or fall below the goals you set for yourself?

Looking past the natural rise and fall that came from market changes, many advisors I ask those questions of tell me they've hit a plateau.

When I talk to a professional who has stalled, I ask a lot of questions about the steps they are taking to elevate their skills. Specifically, I'll ask them if they invest as much time refining their practice management and client acquisition approach as they do studying and refining their professional skills.

More often than not, the client will reveal that he or she is a serious student when it comes to enhancing their knowledge about their core skills, yet are locked in the status-quo when it comes to relationship management and business development. They are basically repeating the same practices but hoping for different results (and I believe they have a term for that).

It's worth asking yourself: "Do I have one year of experience 15 times?"

Comfort is the enemy of achievement - Farrah Gray

In business, we have to be committed to continual refinement and optimization. The velocity of change, the intensity of competition, and the increase in volatility requires that we continually look for ways to elevate our approach and be positioned for anything.

There is so much out of your control in business. When you create a vision for the future and you drive it with specific actions that are within your control, you put the odds in your favor and lower the risk of being at the mercy of things beyond your grasp.

You undoubtedly have some short- and medium-range goals, and also have some *Ideal Life* big-picture goals. These are ultimately what you want to achieve "when I grow up," as one advisor I know puts it. The bottom line is this: If you want your outcomes to change, your actions have to change.

If you want to break the mold, get more fulfillment from your business, and ultimately ride it as a means to an end in others areas of enjoyment in your life, allow me to remind you of three key performance indicators that the perpetually effective and limitless professionals focus on and refine. Keep in mind that these are learned skills. You have some innate skills and qualities that come easy to you, but ultimately everything you need to refine to achieve a breakthrough can be learned.

Communication - One advisor summed up this issue with "I'm good at math but lousy at English."

I'm not trivializing your ability to discuss investment management or provide perspective on market rallies or retreats, or on whatever expertise you possess, but most of your clients empower you to deal with that. They like to know that you know, but they don't need to know everything you know. To paraphrase legendary personal development guru J. Douglas Edwards, 98 percent of success is in understanding people and what they want, while about two percent is product knowledge.

That might be an oversimplification, but I've seen time and time again that there is little correlation between how much someone knows about financial services and how successful they will ultimately be. Often, the key that separates the best from the rest is the ability to communicate effectively.

A personal branding strategy, a compelling value proposition, and well-crafted messaging speaks to people at a deeper level and elevates you from the pack so you are never swimming in that lukewarm pool of sameness.

Run Your Business like a Business - As each year goes by, you want the equity value in your business to increase based on two factors: Your production and your processes.

A process-driven business creates predictability and efficiency. Repeatable procedures create a consistent experience for clients, and that enhances loyalty, empowerment and advocacy. Streamlined systems and a focus on efficiency increase capacity and create liberation, order and scalability.

A top advisor with 300 clients doesn't have 300 different portfolio platforms. Top advisors don't trade time for money by operating out of their heads. Process is the key to higher production, greater profitability and fulfillment and, ultimately, your business is far more valuable when it comes time to sell it.

Client Acquisition Consistency - The lifeblood of your business is the continual revenue generated by your clients. The key is to find a balance between contentment and aspiration.

Top professionals never take their foot off the gas when it comes to client acquisition. For some, this means that their number of clients doesn't change much year-to-year, but the quality is continually progressing.

Natural attrition and occasional right-sizing based on ideal client fit is offset by continually raising the bar that defines an ideal client. This enables you to project scarcity and create an environment where clients appreciate belonging to your community and prospective clients aspire to belong.

For other professionals with more traditional client acquisition goals, they understand the need to put prospective clients into the funnel using a professional, linked and sequential DRIP process - as detailed later - rather than a random "spray and pray" approach. Once in the funnel, a fit process that attracts prospects rather than chasing them ensures that they move from the funnel, into the pipe, and then into your onboarding process. Not only does this ensure that new clients feel accomplished when they come on board (instead of feeling they have been sold something), they are on the fast track to advocacy as well.

The Power of Incrementalism

Albert Einstein called compounding interest the eighth wonder, and one of most powerful forces in the universe. We are all well aware of Rule 72 and how it can work for us when it comes to investing and against us when it comes to borrowing, but it's not just money that compounds; disciplines compound, too.

As a professional productivity coach, I spend a lot of time with clients helping them understand the power of consistent and sequential implementation. When you try to develop a skill such as a second language or a sport, ongoing immersion and refinement over time (rather than a quick bombardment) leads to lasting results.

Often, an advisor will contact us asking if they can attend a weekend seminar or two-day boot camp to improve their productivity and business efficiency. While this type of training can provide a decent introduction to ideas and concepts, it usually won't change habits or lead to lasting results. Silver bullets that provide instant gratification would be nice, but in reality they don't exist.

Incrementalism transcends personal development and affects how you strengthen client relationships. It would be nice if you could take a relationship to a higher level quickly, but that's not how things work. Solid client relationships are based on trust, and trust is earned over time, based on your credentials and chemistry but also because of your consistency and congruency. Your consistent communication – especially an on-going call rotation – compounds over time.

Aristotle said it best: Quality is a habit, not an act. We are what we repeatedly do.

Refer-ability, too, is a by-product of your habits and rituals. The best hour you can spend every day is calling clients and strategic partners. You're not calling to sell anything nor are you trying to be the bearer of any profound news. You are just staying in touch and top-of-mind. You are showing and not merely saying that you value the relationship.

Again, the *Law of Cause and Effect* shows us that, over time, focused, habitual activity always leads to productivity. It's the last five push-ups of the 50 you do that drive home results, which is why you do them all, every time.

Loyalty Fatigue can develop in client relationships, stemming from the *Law of Familiarity*. The more familiar a relationship becomes, the greater the chance your value can be taken for granted or trivialized. Consistent communication will breathe life into your relationships and will not only competitor-proof them, but will create a mindset of predisposition for further investment empowerment and endorsement.

Take Incrementalism One Step Further

You can take an incremental approach to each client conversation you have. Resist the temptation to data-dump information in one long blast and instead take the Socratic approach I have repeatedly referenced by asking your client a question or two and then segueing into your message. Every answer a client provides you effectively gives you permission to go deeper into your messaging.

That is the core of permission marketing – this is where it is born.

Here is an example of permission marketing as it relates to referrals, this one specifically crafted for uncertain or challenging times:

You: *"Mr. Client, how are your friends and family members coping with this period of turbulence and uncertainty? Are they looking to the future with anticipation or apprehension?"*

[Client Responds]

You: *"Mr. Client, if you don't mind me asking, when you talk about me with a friend or family member, what do you say? How do you describe me?"*

[Client Describes You]

You: *"The reason I'm asking you these questions is that I want to remind you about my value-added service that you might find to be useful, especially during these uncertain times. Remember, I make myself available to act as a sounding board for friends and family members of my clients who have questions or concerns about their current financial plan."*

Then continue the conversation by positioning referrals as a *service you provide to them* rather than as a *favor you're requesting of them*.

When you ask questions and sequentially introduce your message, you have a much more engaged client who feels involved in the conversation, rather than being a spectator. Take an incremental approach to your relationship management, personal development, and business refinement and your efforts will compound and give you the results you're looking for.

In the process, you will temper your expectations to be far more realistic and predictable. Stress is born in the gap between expectations and reality. If your expectations are in sync with reality, your stress level will lower considerably, enabling you to focus on solid, productive activities.

That's the power of Incrementalism.

The Loyalty Ladder

Another powerful and effective business-building tool is the concept of the *Loyalty Ladder*. It is easy to understand, foundational to most other business building activities, tremendously powerful, and applicable to nearly every industry.

The loyalty ladder helps you identify your most valuable prospects (MVPs) and focuses your client acquisition efforts on those most likely to convert from prospect to customer. It also charts a course for incremental relationship-building activities and objectives with your existing clientele. The rungs of the ladder include: *Suspect, prospect, customer, client,* and *advocate.* Every single person in your market area resides on one of those five rungs.

You are striving to achieve conversion. Your objective is to convert as many people as possible (at least to your maximum predetermined capacity) all the way through to the top rung of the ladder.

I won't use this section to concentrate on the bottom rungs. Instead, we'll focus on your existing clientele – the top three rungs. Let's quickly define these three. *Customers* do some business with you, but they also do some business with one or more of your competitors. *Clients* empower you fully and do all their business with you, but never send you referrals. *Advocates* are the dream clients. They are fiercely loyal and wave your flag whenever the opportunity arises. They consistently introduce prospective clients to you.

Most professionals fixate on how many clients they can get, when the true goal is how many advocates they can get. That is where the value lies, especially over the long haul.

I talk with many professionals who tell me they have 200 clients. I usually find out in short order that they have something in the neighborhood of 62 customers, 130 clients and eight advocates. Talk about a huge untapped opportunity! Think about the example above and your own business, and consider the impact under the Rule of 52 (The Rule of 52 suggests that every person in your inner circle of clients each has their own inner circle of about 52 friends and family members). What would happen if you went from eight advocates to 50 advocates? That would be a monumental game changer – all without talk of increasing your overall number of relationships!

There is an efficiency component to the Loyalty Ladder, as well. It takes far more time, money and effort to convert a new prospect into a customer or client than it does to convert an existing client into a referral-generating advocate. Stop working so hard at convincing new people, and instead work with people who are already convinced.

You can conduct your own analysis of your implementation of the Loyalty Ladder right now by answering these core questions:

- Is it possible that you have some current customers who aren't aware of all the services you provide?

- Do you currently have a compelling way to convey your full array of offerings in order to convert customers into clients?

- Can you position the concept of full empowerment as a service to your customers rather than as a benefit to you?

- Do you have a clear, replicable process by which to communicate to your clients why, who and how they should be introducing people to you? Are you positioning referrals as a benefit to your advocates rather than as a favor to you?

Wouldn't it be great if your clients not only knew *why* they should refer someone to you but also *who* is a good fit for you? Your understanding of how to clearly communicate all these points and concepts to your clients will grow as you work your way through this book and implement its processes. Putting the pieces into place in your practice provides a foundation for trust, empowerment and refer-ability, and gets customers climbing up your Loyalty Ladder.

Start Your Strategic Plan for Next Year Now

You are probably conscious of gaps that need to be dealt with by now, have crafted your trailer, your personal value proposition and have a basic handle on your branding. Let's climb to the 40,000-foot level and take a strategic look. And before you are tempted to put it off, right now is the ideal time to start bringing your vision for the future out of your head and galvanizing it on paper.

If you patiently and deliberately create a plan for the coming year over the next few months, rather than on a Sunday evening over the holidays in December, you'll create a plan that better serves you as a guidance system, is more actionable and predictable, and consists of goals that are balanced, clear and attainable.

If anyone knows the power of advice and the importance of planning, it's a knowledge-for-profit professional. Think about it, what would you tell someone who told you they don't see the value of professional advice and planning? If they said to you, *"I'm doing it myself because a professional advisor is too expensive and the results can be underwhelming or uncertain."* You'd probably tell them - or at least think to yourself - *"That is ... crazy."* It would be like a person with a tooth-ache deciding to work on their own teeth.

Your plan has to be an ongoing, living process. It's not 'once a year and done'. It won't surprise you that one of my pet peeves in business is centered on the lack of implementation of a strategy. Ideas are a dime a dozen. It is the implementation of an idea that sets it apart from everything else and brings it to life. A plan lets you implement efficiently.

With that said, I admit that when I hear the words "business plan," I often feel a wave of discomfort sweep over me which I have to shake off, perhaps after muttering some foul language under my breath for good measure.

Why the reaction? Consider what happens with about 90 percent of the annual business plans that professional advisors prepare. This is one probable scenario: It is late December and you start to wade through the 20 to 30 pages of the business plan that your company provides for you, and perhaps even requires you to complete. You pick at it over a few weeks, and then, with the deadline looming, you set aside a couple of hours and plow through the document as quickly as you can. A sense of relief rushes over you as click the "save" button and send it off to head office. You may even print a copy which you sit marveling at for a few minutes before you file it away in a drawer, never to be seen again.

Well, at least until year-end when you may use it to help you figure out what to write in the next business plan.

Regardless of my reaction and the "usual scenario" as detailed above, strategic business plans can have real value if they are referred to regularly and adjusted as needed. Are you meeting your targets? What can be done to bring you back on track? What needs to be adjusted in your business activities to ensure the desired outcomes? What changes have to be implemented with your clients?

Reading the plan again can create awareness of your shortfalls, and can ignite a flood of new ideas that can be used to get you back on track for the year. Each new idea requires some planning for implementation, and detailing the necessary steps to be taken to actually bring the idea into fruition within your business, but with your overall plan in place, these will be minor adjustments.

Don't wait until the end of the year. Any time is a perfect time to pull out your strategic plan again and look at it as a jump start - a new beginning, if you will. When I do this, it always seems to me like a second New Years, and I have the opportunity to evaluate what I want to accomplish over the remaining months of the year.

Take a few hours to review what you wrote last year and make some decisions on what adjustments you can and should make right now. I guarantee that reading it again - examining what you wanted to implement, and considering what you actually did - will make a huge difference in the remaining months of this year and, ultimately, for years to come.

Keep your old plans. Every time the document changes, archive what was previously written. Over the course of a year you may end up with three, four, or even five versions of your business plan as it adapts. They become a progression and an evolution. Your course of action can be tracked and accounted for, and your strategic business plan can become an established process for planning and implementation going forward.

Whether you use a business plan template through a CRM, or create your own document yearly on your computer, the most important point is that you take the time to plan, create, update and utilize one.

Perhaps the next time I hear someone talk about a business plan, the conversation will be around how it has become a constant and invaluable reference point for their business, as opposed to something that is filed away and forgotten.

The Power of Consistency and Mid-Course Corrections

Having a plan is a solid start. Carrying it out is what differentiates the actually successful from the potentially successful.

Following a recent seminar where I talked about a proven process that improves client review meetings, an advisor approached me and said, "I really liked a couple of those ideas you shared. I used to do some of that a while back and it worked really well, but then I stopped for some reason."

You can't argue with that logic. You stopped using an idea that worked really well!?

As odd as it may sound, this happens quite often. The ubiquity of "new" ideas that you are exposed to at conferences, from wholesalers, through on-line tips, through books and other sources can be intense and frequent. As one advisor said to me, "I have the attention span of a hummingbird and I love trying new things to add some juice to my business." It's understandable. We're all attracted to shiny new things. The problem is that adding a new idea often comes at the expense of dropping something else before it had a chance to gain meaningful traction.

An extension of this is *The Law of Familiarity* that I referenced earlier. Advisors can get bored with proven strategies and drift off-track, deviating from a tried-and-true process. This often leads to a hitting a plateau and then regressing. This law can also affect clients in such a way that they can develop loyalty fatigue with an advisor of many years, so that the relationship drifts into indifference.

It can be tricky to try to balance consistency with on-going personal and professional development. We've all been to seminars where we hear an idea but dismiss it because we've heard it before, thinking, *"Been there, done that."* We're aware of the merit of the idea but we're not implementing it. In most cases we haven't "done that".

We're not being consistent in how we apply process, despite knowing how important consistency is to building a business and managing relationships. Clients crave consistency because it removes any mystery about how you will conduct yourself. Consistency ensures that any expectation you set will be met and that leads to client satisfaction and loyalty, and ultimately to greater refer-ability. Consistency leads to predictable outcomes, and measurable results.

I'd like to talk briefly about the distinction between deviation and refinement. It's easy to fall into a consistency trap where complacency seeps in. The Japanese have a word - Kaizen - which means 'good change'. The business world has adopted and altered it slightly to mean continuous improvement, and Japanese business in particular sees it as a daily, ongoing process. Being consistent doesn't mean that you shouldn't be open to the refinement of your established procedures. We can always improve the things we do, and we have to do so in a balanced way.

With that in mind, what is your attitude to business advice? Do you continually seek it out to help you break old patterns and self-imposed limits? Are you a serious student when it comes to personal and professional development? Do you focus on what it costs, or on what it's worth?

There are some advisors whose business growth is tied primarily to the natural lift of the markets or another industry. They're not doing anything special or even deliberate when it comes to business development. These are the same advisors who operate in isolation, end up in a vacuum and eventually plateau.

There are other advisors who channel their existing momentum, make continual refinements to proven strategies, address the issues that are undermining their achievement, and document a plan to ensure they continually focus on the things they can control. These advisors go from strength to strength because they have clarity and a planned process.

There are plenty of difficult obstacles in your path. Don't allow yourself to become one of them - Ralph Marsten

That clarity is one of the most important results of having or building a plan and a process. It allows you to tune out the noise and distractions and focus on proven strategies that generate results. A good plan serves as a reminder of what matters as the year unfolds to ensure that you don't drift off track. Ultimately it's about a solid trajectory and mid-course corrections made early.

It's Not the Wind, it's the Set of the Sails

Legendary personal and business development philosopher and speaker Jim Rohn often said the following: "The winds of opportunity blow the same for all of us. The difference that separates the best from the rest is how they set their sails."

As a professional advisor, you invest a lot of time with your clients helping them face the future with confidence thanks to your investment planning process. Be sure that *you* have a plan, and that it's leading you to your goals.

W-5 and Goal-Setting: The Importance of the Moment

*A gem cannot be polished without friction, nor a
man perfected without trials* - Seneca

It might seem odd to start a goal-setting conversation around the importance of gratitude, as referenced in the first "W" point in the W5 Process that follows. Isn't the purpose of setting a goal rooted in achieving something you don't yet have?

While I'm not an authority on psychology, I can say from personal experience that focusing too much on the future can create anxiety, while dwelling too much on the past can cause depression.

I think there is a sweet spot between visions of potential and memories of the past. It's called the moment. Case in point: I was golfing with my son and he was frustrated because we were playing with another kid whose skills were more advanced. My son was sucked into the comparison trap and started getting down on himself. His frustration started stacking and his confidence fell apart in a shattered mess, prompting him to want to quit.

Afterward, we had a conversation and I asked him to savor the moment – if just for a moment. I asked him to listen to the birds, feel the warm breeze and smell the cut grass with a deep breath. Essentially, I was trying to get him to focus on appreciating what he has and where he was at that moment, while still aspiring for what he wanted; to hurry up and get better at golf!

I wanted to make the gulf between where he was and where he wanted to be a little smaller, while not making that the focal point of the moment.

Personal accomplishment is a direction, not a destination. It's never a bad idea while charting a route and following the trail to our goals to adopt an "in the meantime" mindset. While I pursue what I want, I'm going to pay tribute to what I have, and enjoy all the beauty that surrounds me - which could be missed if my focused goal-attainment blinders are on. If you've read Eckart Tolle's book *The Power of Now*, you probably have a deep appreciation for this mindset.

Perspective is vital. I read an article that mentioned that every living creature with a heart will typically have about 2.5 billion heartbeats in its lifetime. Rabbits with high heart rates have a shorter lifespan than a plodding tortoise. When it comes to people, actuaries could share the spectrum of outcomes, but ultimately the heart is a ticking clock. I also recently read that over 100 billion people have lived on earth and that, based on recent history, about 150 million new people will be born and about 50 million will die this year.

I'm not trying to get too cosmic here, but those numbers do add some perspective and proportion to our lives. To me, it just reminds me of the distinction between meaningful wealth and material wealth.

Resilience and its Impact on Gratitude & Humility

People who have stared adversity down typically have immense gratitude.

I have friends who have overcome incredible odds. One in particular likes downplaying his substantial success by saying, "I just kept running into walls until one became a door."

Another deflects from his own resilience and attributes his breakthrough to the people he was around. "I was lucky to be able to draft behind some very talented people who cleared a path for me," he likes to say, and, "I'm like a bright moon and my associates are the sun. The brightness I project is just a reflection of them."

A positive aspect of gratitude is that it helps prevent us from 'selling out' as we pursue our goals. It helps make sure that we don't allow our achievements to come at a cost that was too high in terms of collateral damage. Balance is the goal.

With all that in mind, let me introduce you to the W5 planning process.

The W5 Process

The following process can get your vision for the future out of your head and onto paper in a concrete form. Many advisors have told me that they use this format as a framework for their goal-setting approach with clients with great results, too. It's also very effective to use with kids to get them visualizing a blueprint for the future, while still appreciating the present.

What are you grateful for?

With so much emphasis on the future, it's easy to overlook what we've accomplished up to this point in our lives. Often, the things many professionals are most grateful for and proudest of are challenges overcome.

Your resilience can be a core that attracts people to work with you. Remember, though, that no one is interested in adversity until you've got a story of how you overcame it. A problem solved is a hero's story, rather than a complaint.

The elusive goal of balance suggests that we be both ambitious and content. Gratitude allows you to savor your accomplishments and fuel your aspiration to higher levels. It's a good place to start.

Where do you see yourself in the future?

Be all-encompassing as you create a wish list. Many people focus only on production and income goals, but what is it, ultimately, that makes us valuable in our own estimation? Our personal goals are an important piece of the puzzle, but they are also a means to an end. Write out as many items as you can as you go through this step. Get them out of your head. Try to connect the past to the present as well as the future.

When do you hope to accomplish these goals?

Browse through your wish list and define the items with specific time-lines of 6-month, 1-, 3- and 5-year goals. Then identify one or two that you feel will have the most profound impact on your life when you achieve them.

Why is this so important to you?

This question asks you to drill down and identify your key motivators, things that will drive you to see past the obstacles and adversity that you will face as you strive to achieve your goals.

Who do I need to become to achieve this?

This is heavy question that requires some soul searching. To turn a dream into a reality you'll have to elevate yourself out of your current mold. The results we'll achieve next year won't change much from last year if we don't change, which leads us to the ultimate reality check:

How will I accomplish my goals?

You'll need an action plan to achieve a breakthrough.

We've all fallen for the "Illusion of Skill" that suggests that through talent, perseverance and brute force we can accomplish bigger and better things. It's almost a hint of psychosis, where we keep hammering the same nail assuming something different will happen if we just hit it harder.

Without a guidance system, we tend to drift, or spin our wheels and mistake motion for action. If you want to sell your business for maximum value in three years, you'll have to get the business out of your head and your assistant's head, and create a procedures manual that can lead to predictable, sustainable and duplicable systems that the buyer of your business will pay a premium for. If you want a higher quality and quantity of referrals, you'll need a service matrix to ensure the top 20 percent of your clients get 80 percent of your attention. If you want to simplify your life, you may need to right-size and lay out a process to disassociate yourself from clients that are not a good fit.

That all probably sounds like work to you, but if the "why" is clear and concise, the "how" will get that much easier, and that is the power of a well-rounded goal setting process.

You may already be familiar with Bryan Dyson's great speech on balance, goals and what's of greatest value in life. Dyson, former CEO of Coca Cola™, summed up the issue better than anyone else I am familiar with:

"Imagine life as a game in which you are juggling some five balls in the air. You name them – Work, Family, Health, Friends and Spirit and you're keeping all of these in the air.

"You will soon understand that work is a rubber ball. If you drop it, it will bounce back. But the other four balls – Family, Health, Friends and Spirit – are made of glass. If you drop one of these; they will be irrevocably scuffed, marked, nicked, damaged or even shattered. They will never be the same. You must understand that and strive for it.

"Work efficiently during office hours and leave on time. Give the required time to your family, friends and have proper rest. Value has a value only if its value is valued."

The Balance between Ambition and Contentment

Ambition gets a bad rap at times, and it shouldn't.

The foundation of pure ambition is rooted in absolute gratitude. Putting some proportion to your existing success and the concept of your vision for the future must be balanced by humility and appreciation for your accomplishments, both in your nature and in what you've nurtured.

If you travel around the world, you don't have to go too far to realize that most of the people on the planet would kill for your worst day. Because you aspire to achieve things through integrity-centered actions, you accomplish goals through the service of others rather than at the expense of others. So keep on dreaming big dreams but, in the meantime, be happy with what you've already accomplished while you aspire to fill in the boxes that have yet to be checked.

The *Law of Reciprocity* suggests that giving starts the receiving process. You could say that's just another way of describing Karma. The problem with Karma is that it's not an exact science because of the reality of time. Karma always works - eventually - but not always in line with our schedule. So it's not a bad idea to detach from any expectation of outcome and productivity and just stay true to fundamentally solid and integrity-based activity. Your legacy and sense of purpose will appreciate it.

"Fire Your Coach!"

Sometimes a coach can be an asset in achieving your goals, but not always. External advice can impact what you are accomplishing, but it can simultaneously undermine who you are becoming.

I had a conversation with a professional advisor who informed me that he was interested in hiring us to deploy practice management systems and procedures within his business. During the process, he revealed that he also recently hired a coach who was to help him improve his sales skills so that he could "close more deals."

He was a bit startled when I said to him that the only way we could work together is if he were to fire his other coach.

My logic was simple; the tactics taught by a sales coach were not aligned with our philosophy and approach and would ultimately undermine the advisor's long term goals.

Again, professional client acquisition and retention does not involve salesmanship. It revolves around how you are perceived and described.

Define Yourself or You are Automatically Defined

We talked about this in the preceding branding section, but let me elaborate: How do you want to be perceived by a prospective client? As broker selling investments, or as a professional providing a process and client-centered solutions? How do you want to be described by your clients when they have an opportunity to shine a light on you?

Many people still think of professional advisors as salespeople on commission. Your actions on a daily basis will either validate that or prove them wrong. This is why I spend a lot of time deprogramming our advisor clients and replacing their sales approach with a consultative approach. That shift allows them to implement a service model that ensures their clients focus on what the advisor is worth, rather than what he or she costs. You need to be a shepherd, not a hunter-gatherer.

I talk to advisors all the time - some of whom seem to be in a trance as they unconsciously demonstrate their mindset of salesmanship. It reveals a lot when an advisor says things like:

"When I meet a prospect they are as good as closed."

"When I get a referral I always ask the client, 'Who else do you know?'"

"I eat what I kill."

Don't misinterpret what I'm saying here. I don't want to come off as idealist, elitist or disrespectful. From a practical perspective, our clients have proven time and time again that their persuasive impact has soared by adopting our stewardship approach. Not only do you avoid looking needy or desperate when it comes to new ideal client acquisition, you attract new business instead of chasing it.

Clearly you don't want to be perceived as a hunter/gatherer. You want prospects to sell *you* on becoming *your* client. Clients who will come to you with new needs as new money goes in motion. Clients who will steer new people your way, because they feel they are doing their friend a disservice by not making the introduction. Finally, clients never leave you because of the professional proactive and unexpected service you provide.

The affluent client is becoming increasingly enlightened and savvy when it comes to the transparency of fees and the value they expect. The smart advisor knows that the relationship lasts long after initial commissions are spent. Commissions alone can be anticlimactic. Recurring revenues, predictable referrals and additional empowerment ensure the honeymoon will never be over.

To focus on your value from a client's viewpoint requires three key elements: A plan, a process and an understanding of how everything you do reflects on how you are perceived. It requires integrating all these things into your strategic planning. If you want to drill down even further, the STAR process will help you hit all three targets.

Bringing It All Together: A S.T.A.R. is Born

You'll be glad to know that I'm not going to suggest that you now create an exhaustive document that will take all sorts of time and effort and that you'll probably never look at again after you've finished creating it. When I coach a professional advisor, I ideally want to help them create a four-page plan that serves as a snapshot for what they want to achieve, how they can achieve it and outlines a guidance system that will serve them as the year unfolds.

There are a lot of external dependencies that have to cooperate for a new year to run smoothly. With talk of an unpredictable economy, tax changes, global uncertainty and unrest, it's possible that the next few years are going to be as turbulent as the past few. You can't predict all the headwinds and issues that will interfere with your plans, and, frankly, there's always *something* on the horizon.

There are four basic pieces to the strategic planning and branding puzzle, and if you put these pieces together and hard-wire the concepts into your day-to-day approach, it is conceivable that, like a tractor beam, you can attract virtually any goal you set. I use the simple acronym S.T.A.R. for the outline. S.T.A.R. represents the four pieces of your planning blueprint:

- **Self-Analysis**– to complement your gap analysis
- **Targets** – to get clarity on the goals you want to achieve
- **Activities** – which you will implement to achieve your productivity goals
- **Reality Check** – to keep you on track and ensure you don't drift

S: Self-Analysis

Before you consider a single planning activity, it is critical that you conduct, for lack of a better term, a personal state of the nation. Think of it this way; over the years, you've probably done a lot of things right and you've probably misfired a few times. The key is to invest your past into your future and to tighten up your overall approach. This is implementation of the *Law of Optimization*.

The self-analysis process is a way to make some critical observations about your business. An obvious first look is to identify your untapped opportunities. Like veins of gold lying dormant within your business, these opportunities could and should be harvested. Untapped opportunities relate to under-utilized client acquisition possibilities.

The next observation is in gaining clarity with respect to your overlooked vulnerabilities. These are the issues that are undermining you and have caused you to plateau. Every professional advisor I have met possesses both untapped opportunities and overlooked vulnerabilities.

A good early point is to determine who your MVPs are. A prospect hierarchy exists, and it is important to identify your Most Valued Prospects. As always, it is more important to reach people who count than it is to count the number of people you reach. You might discover that your most valued prospects are in fact clients who are holding assets elsewhere. You might have potential promotional partners, such as accountants and lawyers, with whom you could collaborate. Perhaps you have a client within a demographic or socioeconomic target market that you could work with to establish a new target market or prospecting pillar?

In almost every case, however, your most valued prospects are the friends and family members of your existing clients, and with a little focus you could improve the frequency of client endorsements. Examine your business and identify your MVPs. It is a vital step in taking your business to the next level.

Once you've gained clarity in terms of your opportunities, shift gears and scrutinize your business to uncover your vulnerabilities. Your clients are being hit by your competitors now more than ever. As I've mentioned, a natural loyalty fatigue can develop among long-term clients stemming from the *Law of Familiarity*. Do you have some relationships that you might be taking for granted? Have you taken the steps necessary to competitor-proof those relationships? The industry is changing at a rapid clip, with the products and services you provide being commoditized more every day, and now would be a good time to identify your unique value proposition in order to differentiate yourself and insulate your business from forces beyond your control.

Here are some questions you can ponder as you're taking a deeper dive into your own personal gap analysis:

- *Why is the quality of referrals I get not in sync with the quantity?*
- *Why is it a one-way street with Centers of Influence?*
- *What would happen if my assistant left tomorrow?*
- *Do my clients fully understand what I do and all that I can provide?*
- *Have I done a good job competitor-proofing my clients?*
- *What systems can I put in place to improve consistency and predictability?*
- *What issues cause me stress that I should be addressing in my life?*
- *Am I prepared if the world decides to go crazy again as it did in 2008?*

Some advisors misinterpret this process as being negative or paranoid. I'm an optimistic person by nature, but management guru Peter Drucker reminds us to respect the *Reality Principle* that says we must deal with things as they are, not as we wish them to be. Andy Grove, one of the founders of Intel, wrote a book entitled *Only the Paranoid Survive* in which he reminds us that a positive power can stem from what some might consider negative thinking. For example, you would never wait for the oil light to come on in your car before you checked the engine.

Sometimes, cautious concern is the wise choice. Take the same approach with your business. A little preventative maintenance along with some candid scrutiny can reveal necessary minor adjustments that will lead to major improvements

T: Targets and Goals

Once you've completed your self-analysis, the next logical step is to clarify your targets and goals. It probably comes as no surprise to you that when I ask advisors for their goals, most either don't have any, or their goals are strictly financial in nature.

As I documented earlier in the W5 process, you must set goals that extend into all areas of your life. That is when your true motivators are uncovered, and you establish your sense of purpose. Purpose is stronger than object-oriented goals alone and just as important as process. The guidance system that stems from your sense of purpose is even more powerful than a correct business strategy, and it goes a long way toward helping you see past the setbacks and short-term obstacles that will be present along your journey. Your sense of purpose is your beacon. It affects every decision you make and shapes your character, and few things are more attractive than a strong character.

Don't get me wrong. Making money and establishing financially related goals (especially when it comes to productivity) are essential, but I suggest you go well beyond, and here's why; at the end of the day, money doesn't make you valuable. It's not what you get in life that makes you valuable, it's what you become. Your purpose in life is what shapes your legacy. Often this reminder is what rejuvenates someone to focus more on the things they love, and creates a sense of fulfillment.

It's hard to excel at something you don't love doing and sometimes the less desirable aspects of the job can seep in and distort the areas that matter to you.

This is especially important when you consider that true success is incremental and takes time to gather momentum. Without clearly stated goals, it's easy to lose focus and drift off course. While your trajectory can be flexible, your destination should be fixed. All entrepreneurs need to improvise and tinker with their approach as the year unfolds, as long as those improvisations take them closer to their goals.

Clarify your goals on paper. Use the W-5 Process. You can't just randomly or haphazardly approach the future; you must design it. You've heard about the fool who goes hunting with a crossbow and fires an arrow into the forest, saying to himself, "Boy, I sure hope something runs into that." Later, he finds the arrow lodged into a tree and draws a bull's eye around it.

Don't leave your future to chance.

A: Activities

We'll delve into this in a lot more detail; at this point I want to sort through some of your activity priorities at a basic level.

The *Law of Cause and Effect* states that your activities determine your productivity; but not all activities are created equal. Some activities have a greater measurable impact on your business than others. The Pareto Principle applies here. I'll say it again: One issue that separates the best advisors from the rest is that the best don't major in minor activities. As Hemingway said, "You can't mistake motion for action."

So what are the activities that will give you the highest return on your investment of time and capital?

There are activities that you *could* do, activities that you *should* do, activities that you *must* do, and finally the activities that you ultimately *will* do. You need to implement the activities that you must do based on your observations during the self-analysis. For example, an advisor who receives few referrals from their five hundred clients should not engage in prospecting activities. All their efforts should be focused on their existing clientele rather than trying to attract new ones.

A lot of people in your market area need your expertise, but you shouldn't spend time with people who need you at the expense of people who deserve you. You are only one person with just 24 hours in a day. Work with the people who are already convinced and let them convince their acquaintances for you.

This brings us to the importance of focus. When it comes to business development, you have to remember who your MVPs are and focus your efforts there. Again, the most important prospects you have are the friends and family members of your clients. It's all about reducing friction, so before you start trying to convince new people, you should work more closely with the people who are already convinced. Deploy a professional referral process that positions the concept of you meeting with a friend of a client as service you are providing them rather than as a favor you are asking of them. Consistently communicate your value on an on-going basis.

Your next best MVPs are actually some of your clients. These are customers who don't empower you fully and do business with other financial providers. Have you deployed a process to communicate your full array of services to your clients positioned as a benefit to them rather than as a selling opportunity? Do you continually discuss their unmet needs as their lives unfold and new money moves into motion?

Another solid group of MVPs are the clients of your strategic partners. Have you leveraged your client relationships properly to get closely acquainted with their other professional service providers? Do you have existing relationships with Centers of Influence, but unfortunately they are one-way-street relationships? This is a massive untapped opportunity that can be addressed through a methodical, sequential approach, and I'll expand on this in depth later in this book.

Your last MVPs are pure target markets. We'll get into this in more detail later on, as many professionals don't do any organized prospecting. Demographic, geographic, socioeconomic and vertical sector target markets are available to you. The first place to look to establish a target market is where you already have momentum. Do you have a group of existing clients in a specific area such as entrepreneurs, professionals, or groups based on shared interests that you could target and expand?

Most marketing activities fall within two categories: Ongoing activities and time-line activities. Since 80 percent of your productivity stems from 20 percent of your activities, my suggestion is that you first become incredibly effective at implementing the activities that fall in the "20 percent" category. Those activities are usually ongoing in nature and they relate to your daily code of conduct. In other words, "moments of truth" present themselves to you each and every day when clients reveal something of importance to you (and much more on this, later). Your responses to those brief windows of opportunity make up your code of conduct and have a tremendous impact on your business.

Let me give a quick example regarding moments of truth by way of an analogy. If you play golf you know that it can take as long as five hours to play a round. During that five hours, how much time do you spend actually hitting the golf ball? Chances are, about 90 seconds. Everything else you do on the golf course contributes to your score, but the moments of truth are those 90 seconds that you actually spend striking the ball. In a typical business day, you have a few fleeting moments of truth as well. It's important to do things right, but it is more important to do the right things that make a statement and demonstrate that you are paying attention.

How do you welcome new clients? How do you say thank you for client referrals? How do you respond to client service issues? Do you recognize milestones? As a business owner, branding is everything to your business, and everything you do is part of your branding. Everything you do *matters*. Scrutinize the entire client experience, and make a list of how you will respond to moments of truth. This is the first step in creating velocity, building confidence and ensuring that you are continually refining and optimizing your systems and procedures. Everything has to be rooted in process and habits.

If, after mastering ongoing activities, you still find yourself with time on your hands, consider plugging appropriate time-line activities into your marketing plan calendar. These represent monthly and/or quarterly activities such as seminars, newsletters, target marketing campaigns and the like. Perhaps you will roll out a client advisory council for your favorite 15 clients. Maybe you'll implement a client profiling campaign to gather important Family, Occupational and Recreation information to enhance the chemistry you are creating with your best clients. Perhaps you'll send out Thanksgiving cards next fall and a line extension campaign next spring aimed at uncovering hidden assets to ensure you are your clients' lead provider of financial services.

R: Reality Check

The final piece of the puzzle is the reality check. Review your action plan and it should answer an important question: What kind of person do I need to become in order to make this plan a reality? What books do I need to read, what people do I need to collaborate with, what skills and qualities do I need to refine, and what do I need to do differently in order to translate my potential into actual results?

As an action-oriented entrepreneur, you know that if things are going to change, you need to change. You can have a plan chock full of great ideas, but ideas aren't the issue. Execution is the key. You could e-mail your plan to 50 of your closest competitors without a worry in the world because most people stay locked in the status quo. Understanding this concept is the master key that separates the best from the rest and unlocks one's true potential.

Never before has this been more important. The rate of change in nearly every industry is dizzying. To be current is not enough. You must continually drive obsolescence into a small corner and find new ways to make your business and yourself more attractive to the marketplace. The best advice I've ever received in my life is that income will rarely exceed self-development. The best way to attract great clients is to make yourself more attractive by continually sharpening your skills. Like all laws in life, if you follow the *Law of Attraction,* people will follow you. In other words, you must commit to being a serious student. If you want to earn more, you must learn more. But don't just study the markets, study marketing too. Consistent business development must be a core competency or you'll be left by the side of the road.

I know of professional advisors who have transformed their entire businesses after having read *The Millionaire Next Door.* I know others still who have tightened their businesses up dramatically and developed airtight systems that allow them to take more time off since reading *The E-Myth.* (As you can tell by now, I'm a big fan of Michael Gerber's book.)

Surround yourself with achievers and cultivate relationships you can profit from. I am constantly urging my clients to target the best and collaborate with the best people they can. Go where the demands and expectations are high, not just for what it gets you but, most importantly, for what it makes of you. Top people act like a tuning fork, helping you to continually hone your skills and your business.

A good plan gives you a panoramic view of your future and has as much pull as the Law of Gravity. Putting a plan together and using it as your guidance system throughout the year will put the odds in your favor and could lead to a breakthrough, making next year your best year ever.

A Break-out Year: Putting Your Strategy into Practice

One of my favorite quotes, often attributed to Confucius, is "Dig your well before you're thirsty." As a professional advisor you know all about the importance of planning, risk management and the power of compounding. From a business perspective, do you apply the same mindset? If you want to have a tremendous next year, the best way to do that is to carry as much momentum forward from this year as you can, compounding your velocity.

I'm reminding you of this because in my recent conversations with many professional advisors, a large number seem to be dwelling on things out of their control, and are pessimistic about the future. I'm suggesting that rather than playing defense, take the contrarian's approach and look at ways to stir the pot right now.

Did you know that construction on the Empire State building began in 1930? This was, for a long time, the tallest building in the world and it was built during a depression. I'm asking you to apply that same vision, confidence and work ethic to your business and build something that stands above the pack, even in periods of uncertainty and volatility.

Don't Reinvent the Wheel

The foregoing doesn't mean that now is the time to dabble or experiment with untested ideas and concepts. There are a lot of 'spray and pray' marketing concepts that are costly, time consuming and ineffective. Let me take you through specific example, a tried-and-true approach that numerous elite advisors have relied on to ensure a solid quarter.

The following is a proven process consisting of actionable strategies that you can implement and translate into results quickly and predictably. I've written about variations of this approach on several occasions but the framework here can be fleshed out to match your unique situation and the time of year. It's an example of implementing the processes this book talks about.

Step 1 – The Call Rotation

Make a list of your top 50 to 100 clients and put them into a 90-day call rotation. You aren't trying to be the bearer of any profound news, you are just touching base to check in with them after the summer/holidays/etc. to see how they are doing.

Use F.O.R.M. as your guide when you ask questions about their family, occupation and recreational interests. Make relevant and timely comments about money and markets. F.O.R.M. helps you *Listen to Learn* instead of *Listen to Respond*. Salespeople tend to process a response as they are listening to someone in order to shape the conversation to suit their needs. Consultants have no hidden agenda and listen to understand the person better; to establish chemistry and determine if there might be an alignment of interests.

As the conversation begins to wind down, ask them this question (you should remember the heart of this from the section on the power of incrementalism):

"How are your friends and family coping with (their expressed concerns/ current industry concerns/other worries)? Are they looking to the future with anticipation or apprehension?"

Their response will last anywhere between 10 seconds and 10 minutes. Encourage them to elaborate. Many core issues are two or three questions deep. Follow-up with this next question:

"If you don't mind me asking, when you talk about me with a friend or family member, what do you say? How do you describe me?"

This series of questions is rooted in Permission Marketing. The answers your clients provide give you permission to remind them of your value proposition:

"The reason I'm asking you these questions is because I want to remind you about a value added service that I provide for my best clients that many find to be very useful. Specifically, I make myself available to act as a sounding board for friends and family members of my clients. Now I'm not asking you to think of anyone right now, this is for down the road. If a friend ever asks about me or you feel compelled to introduce someone to me, simply call me to get the wheels in motion and I will make myself available to address their concerns. And please understand they do not need to become a client to take advantage of this service."

Not to be a broken record, but this disarming statement positions the concept of you meeting with a friend as a service you are *providing* rather than a favor you are *asking* of your clients. You are planting a seed and opening a topic of conversation without projecting any neediness.

If their response is lukewarm or disinterested, you can stop at this point and revisit the topic in a future conversation. You've planted the seed. If they are receptive or inquisitive, you can take a deeper dive and explain a little bit more in detail. A common response from clients is: *"I wasn't aware that you provided this service."*

Respond as follows (and here is where we build off your survey data and the *listening* I talked about, earlier – what has been revealed you can and should point to, continually):

"The reason I do this is because I became a professional advisor to help people make informed decisions with their financial future. It's very fulfilling. One of two things typically occurs when a friend or family member goes through this process. Either I validate for them that their current approach is fundamentally solid, or I reveal a few minor flaws that they might want to consider adjusting. And as you know, minor adjustments can often lead to major improvements down the road. But either way, if they are a friend or family member of yours, I will make myself available and ensure that this is a great investment of their time."

Here are five key points to hit in this conversation:

1. Express your sense of purpose as a professional advisor to validate why you are doing this.

2. Project clarity so that your client knows exactly how an endorsement like this will reflect on them in the eyes of their friends.

3. Replace the word "referral" with "introduce."

4. Replace the words "second opinion" with "sounding board process."

5. Be certain that they know that you won't be trying to sell their friend on becoming a client. There may or may not be a fit in the future but that isn't the point in providing this service.

You want your clients to be in the habit of freely introducing people to you as the opportunity presents itself. Based on the *Law of Cause and Effect*, the activity of meeting people will most certainly lead to productivity down the road.

Will Your Clients be Ready?

There is a concept in marketing referred to as the *Stage of Readiness*. You don't know when a friend or family member will be ready to listen to a client of yours brag about you. The foregoing process ensures that when it does happen, your client will be ready to describe you clearly and persuasively. That said, when your clients are around their friends and family members, especially in the holiday season, potential lines of communication multiply. At parties, dinners and other social gatherings, this process will ensure that when the topic of money comes up, it will be a knee-jerk reaction for your clients to wave your flag.

Once you've deployed this simple and proven strategy, stay consistent. The call rotation must become a habit. Pick your spots to remind your clients about your value added service. To quote Confucius again, "Water dripping on a stone will eventually make a mark."

Every "drip" triggers that moment of recognition and awareness in your clients' minds and keeps you front and center. More than that, a consistent and proactive communication plan also competitor-proofs your clients by strengthening the trust they have in you and your team.

Step 2 – Send Your Best Clients a Thanksgiving Card

As I noted briefly earlier, a Thanksgiving card is a unique and stand-out way to have an impactful contact with a client. The better the card, the more impact it will have, to the point that your clients will have a tough time bringing themselves to throw it out after the holiday has passed. You can go to our website to look over the cards we use to get a better feel for the quality you should aim for.

You are encouraged to put this phrase in the cards you send:

We would like to wish you and your family all the best for the Thanksgiving holiday. We'd also like to thank you for a great relationship.

Use your gathered F.O.R.M. data to pinpoint important dates or events for your Triple-A clients and schedule a related card or focused gift, too.

Step 3 – Send Your Best Clients a Holiday "State of the Nation" Letter

This letter can be enclosed in a holiday card or sent as a stand-alone. It could come along with a calendar, another tangible that has great impact and shelf-life. This letter isn't designed to be an analysis of the markets or a detailed outlook for the future. Instead, it's a statement of what you learned throughout the year and how you will be investing the past into the future.

Put a bigger emphasis on the messenger rather than the message. Share some details of how your family will be spending the holidays. Connect with your clients on a more personal level. You are a leader and you want to convey that.

Finally, you should add this PS at the bottom of the letter:

"Now would also be a great time for me to thank my clients for introducing me to their friends and family members throughout the year. This is a tremendous compliment and a huge responsibility and something I will never take lightly."

The postscript is the most vividly read component of a letter. It is the best place to put a gentle reminder of your call-to-action without putting your clients on the spot.

Visit **www.TheAdvisorPlaybook.com** for access
to the Playbook Implementation Program

Section 3: Branding

How Your Sense of Purpose and a Proprietary Approach Make You Referable

What will undo any boundary is the awareness that it is our vision and not what we are viewing that is limited - James P. Carse

Because of its importance, I want to come back to branding and start talking about ways to integrate your value proposition and your trailer within your overall branding strategy.

As a business development consultant, I am often asked to critique a business owner's value proposition, mission statement or elevator speech. More often than not, my first observation is that the individual's attempt sounds much like everyone else. Even though they use words like "unique" and "differentiate", ultimately the communication is interchangeable, bland and easy to dismiss. Furthermore, the focus tends to be more on *"What I do"* and *"How I do it"*, with little emphasis on *"Why I do it"*.

Your process and professionalism are key components in being attractive to high quality clients, but your purpose is just as important as your process.

It's time for a deeper dive into the art of articulating your value. And it *is* an art – it's the verbal extension of your branding strategy and will color all aspects of your communication with clients.

This art is especially important when it comes to refer-ability. In order to increase the volume and quality of endorsements you receive, it doesn't matter what you believe. What matters is that your clients and partners *believe what you believe.* Unless, and until they do, their ability to relay your value persuasively to someone else will be hampered.

To repeat that old marketing truism: *Facts tell, stories sell.* This has never been more applicable than today as the commoditization of knowledge-for-profit professions continues to accelerate. Your value proposition has to be interesting and engaging. To achieve that, when you are communicating your value, you have to put as much emphasis on you, the messenger, as you do the message. The services and solutions you provide are the message, but *you* are the messenger and you are unique. That's what people lock into, and is what differentiates you from the pack.

In my travels, I've noticed an undeniable trend that supports all of this. When it comes to referrals, there are only two camps: The advisors who effortlessly attract referrals and build a business with second, third and even fourth generation clients and a second group that consists of advisors who hit a plateau and can't seem to get off the client-acquisition treadmill. My goal has been to determine what distinguishes these two groups. While there are several distinctions and similarities, the common thread is that the most referable professional advisors have a clearly defined sense of purpose and they communicate it consistently to their clients and strategic partners.

The question is this: Do your clients know *why* they should refer someone to you? Have you communicated why you will make yourself available to speak to a friend or family member of theirs? Are you clear as to why your clients aren't referring people to you now?

Drive the concept of a referral with your sense of purpose. Use a personalized variation of this scripting, which should be familiar to you by now:

"Let me tell you why I make myself available to be a sounding board for a friend or family member of a client. I became a professional advisor to help people make informed decisions with their financial affairs. Financial success is a matter of choice, not chance. I like helping people make informed choices. Frankly, this is the most fulfilling part of my job. Bottom line is this, if they are important to you, they are important to me. And you can hold me accountable that they will view this process as a tremendous investment of their time. And, as you know, a friend or family member does not need become a client to take advantage of this service"

When you position the concept of a referral as a service you provide rather than as a favor you seek, and then drive it home with your sense of purpose, refer-ability is amplified. You don't look needy and your value is easy to describe to others.

You've seen the idea of clear communication of purpose repeatedly in this book, and it should exist, repeatedly, in your communications with your clients.

Richard Branson, the legendary founder of the Virgin Group of companies, has provided us with many memorable quotes, but the one that supports the power of purpose best is this: "Business has to enhance people's lives or it's simply not worth doing." You enrich lives based on your philosophy and process. It's meaningful and it matters. When you communicate the fulfillment you get from delivering value to someone, you stand out from the pack, you are memorable, and you are more referable.

I caution you, though; not everyone will get it. As Oscar Wilde said, "A cynic is someone who knows the cost of everything and the value of nothing." Don't let the cynics dictate your approach. Find the people who share and value your approach and who have an alignment of interests with you. These are the people who embrace you so completely that they feel they are doing a friend a disservice by not introducing them to you.

Branding and Marketing 2.0

Professional advisors frequently ask me which marketing strategies are best for client acquisition. While there is a place for some marketing strategies and campaigns, often I will steer the conversation toward discussing the power of branding and why it can be more effective than traditional marketing over the long haul.

To repeat myself: Marketing is *selling* something, branding is *building* something.

Traditional marketing tends to be campaign-driven and doesn't have the staying power of branding, which is on-going and part of your habits and rituals. To use the universe as a metaphor, marketing is a shooting star – showy but fleeting. Branding is a sun – something that endures and illuminates.

As a professional advisor, insurance consultant or any other client-service professional, your skills are the driving force for your business. Much of your business is intangible. That can be abstract and there are a lot of things that will always remain outside your control. Branding helps take the abstract nature of what you do and make it easier to understand and appreciate for a client.

That being said, all of your communications take time to sink in and be absorbed. Remember that your MVPs already have another professional service provider. You are trying to position yourself as "No. 2" and create a nagging feeling that they should consider their options. With existing clients, you want to competitor-proof those relationships, gain their full empowerment as unmet needs become apparent and earn their endorsements, bringing them into a full advocate role; but earning advocacy takes time.

Nevertheless, there are ways to encourage and reinforce the evolution from client to advocate.

Telling your story

Advocacy is enhanced when you make it easy for your clients and partners to talk about you.

Using tangible items and imagery is a potent tool that encourages that communication. One simple example of this – this specific one for financial professionals - is the use of coins in your client communications.

I'm not suggesting you get in the gift-giving business, but I am suggesting you go from vapor to paper – or in this example, silver – and use symbols that people can hold in their hands, symbols that take the abstract nature of your value and turn it into something the client can conceptualize and which has lasting shelf-life. I know of several advisors who now send a sterling silver dollar in a handsome case to pay tribute to a client who has referred a friend or family member. The coin is symbolic, and the client can touch it. Money and investing has become so virtual that holding the coin snaps clients out of their fog and reminds them that money can be tangible and beautiful. A symbol like this has immense shelf-life and anchors your relationship every time they look at it.

Building on that, if you want to position yourself in the hearts and minds of the next generation – and throughout your clients' entire family trees for that matter – you can send your clients' children a penny, beautifully framed with a reminder of the power of compounding noted on the back, as a birthday gift. You have undoubtedly seen the example of how a penny that compounds in value every day is worth over a million dollars after 30 days. It's a great metaphor to help a child understand the value of money and the power of the Rule of 72.

There are advisors who have made themselves indispensable to their clients, and created incredible buzz throughout families, by creatively bringing value to their clients' children when it comes to understanding money and investing. If you read *The Millionaire Next Door* by Tom Stanley, you already know the power of positioning yourself within the entire family.

Some of these advisors have paper currency framed in their offices from countries ravaged by hyper-inflation. It is a conversation piece that can help you segue into a financial planning solution you provide.

These are just a few of the nearly infinite, tangible branding ideas available. They are simple and impactful but also remind you and your clients of the importance of what you do. Your legacy and purpose is tied directly to the value you bring people. The key is to inject some personality and creativity into your branding so that you aren't swimming in the pool of sameness with countless other advisors who are hard to remember and easy to dismiss.

Doing so in a way that links your service to the client's family concerns (gathered by your F.O.R.M. process) makes it that much more effective.

Make Yourself Indispensable: Help Your Clients Help Their Kids

One of the easiest and most powerful branding strategies you can deploy to exceed the expectations of your high net-worth clients - and make yourself indispensable to them in the process - is to adopt a train-the-trainer mindset. Help them to encourage their children to develop a solid financial philosophy and approach.

Many first-generation financially independent people make the lives of their children incredibly easy. These self-made, affluent people worked hard and sacrificed to achieve their goals, but they often don't hand down the same work ethic or delayed gratification mindset to the next generation. As a result, many of these kids develop a sense of entitlement and have difficulty overcoming adversity on their own later in life.

You are in a unique position to help counter that.

What's in it For You?

Tom Stanley noted that when money is in motion from one generation to the next, often the first thing that happens is that it leaves the professional advisor. The person inheriting the money often has no relationship with their parents' advisor and, as a result, the assets flow out. Just as Under Armour stole market share from Nike and several jeans manufacturers stole business from Levi Strauss, if you don't have an established relationship with the next generation, you are on a course toward a shrinking client base.

What's in it For Your clients?

Many affluent, self-made people I speak with express concern that maybe they've made things too easy for their kids. Fancy dinners out, exotic vacations, extravagant birthday parties and gifts set some lofty expectations. Coupled with our acceleration toward a cashless society, the concept of the value of money is becoming abstract to kids. As the world gets smaller and billions of eager BRIC nation residents enter the global economy, you have to wonder how prepared western kids are going to be to compete and thrive.

It is safe to say that you have clients that worry about things like this. Chances are you might have a few who worry about their legacy, too. If their kids aren't good with money, will the inheritance vaporize after the shopping spree? It's one thing for the money to evaporate, but so too does all the effort that led to the accumulated wealth.

Look at it this way – the fastest growing sector in the world of psychotherapy is millennials. They are (in)famous for not always being as prepared for reality as they perhaps should be. To stick with the psychological theme, how did Freud start off analyzing a patient? He dug down to their trauma. For your clients, who are worried they haven't passed along the qualities they have developed in their financial success to the next generation, the trauma lies there, and that's something you can help with. That's where you can show your value to a client in a new way.

There are countless inexpensive ways you can make a connection with the next generation and garner goodwill and loyalty from your clients. Here are a few:

Send a copy of *The Richest Man in Babylon* along with a congratulatory card to kids who are graduating. George Clason, who incidentally coined the phrase 'Pay Yourself First', wrote this book back in the 1920s and it still stands up today. In keeping with the mantra that facts tell, but stories sell, this is a great story that engages the reader with the fundamentals.

Send a silver dollar to children on their birthday along with a nice card and perhaps steer them to a good website or YouTube video that talks about the power of saving and investing as well as the perils of debt.

Conduct seminars for kids on the importance of being good with money. Make it fun with games, good food and drinks and prizes.

Create a dedicated social media presence that your clients can steer their kids (and their friends) toward; one that provides tips, links and insights. Have contests and prizes to engage them further.

This is just a sampling of ideas. I don't want you to think I'm being overly idealistic here. These initiatives can have a substantial impact on your branding and a measurable impact on your bottom line. This approach is a bridge that makes it easy for your clients to introduce you to their friends and family members. It makes you attractive, referable and unique and lays the groundwork for multi-generational business.

Right now I can hear some readers saying "that's all great, but I need to know how to reach new clients as well, not just the kids of my existing ones." Before you pull out your elevator speech in your next social encounter, consider the following.

The Anti-Elevator Speech

The 'elevator speech' is a sales technique that has been around an awfully long time. If you want to have a consultative practice where referrals are the norm, though, it might be wise to abandon some of the sales approaches that were imprinted onto our psyche from day one in the business. The elevator speech is one of those approaches.

Take a moment and refer back to the *Let's Shoot Your Trailer* section of this book. That activity, though focused on the client, can also help you solidify and perfect your anti-elevator speech.

For an advisor seeking to attract an affluent clientele, the notion that I can compel or predispose someone to become my client because of some snappy banter upfront is unlikely at best. I've heard professionals many times, and in various social situations, attempt to do this very thing. As an observer, it seemed that if they accomplished anything, it was probably turning the listener off and inspiring them to seek better conversation elsewhere.

The irony of it is that people are attracted to things that they cannot have, or that are hard to get. Why do we work so hard to chase with the elevator speech, when we should be working on trying to attract, instead? If you think about it, the elevator speech (and a lot of classic salesmanship) goes against basic human nature.

Further, although the words have been prettied up greatly, the elevator speech announces to the world that you are on the prowl for clients. This is not attractive to me. Is it to you? This is, at heart, an application of the *Law of Supply and Demand*. What do you supply? Ultimately it's your time, so you need a way to make sure people value that, and find it attractive.

What is the alternative to the elevator speech? This is a recurring situation, in a variety of business and social interactions. We are asked what we do for a living. How can you best make your answer compelling and attractive?

You must paint a picture, in as few words as possible, that describes your business in a way that the listener wants to be a part of. You do it in a natural way, in the appropriate social setting, and it is integrated and constant. You know it backward and forward. You deliver it, and you then stop talking about it. Instead, you start asking that person questions about their life and their business. Trust me, even if you don't say another word because the person is telling you their entire life story, they will recall you later as that amazing conversationalist at the party. You know, the one with the exclusive advisory practice?

An example of some anti-elevator phraseology follows. This is a conversational supplement to your concrete value proposition and can eventually segue to your trailer:

"Oh, well. I am a Professional advisor. I have a practice in town here that intentionally has a smallish number of very terrific clients, and you know, ever since I started working with people that I like, it's a lot more rewarding for me, it's more exclusive, and I am really enjoying some terrific relationships with my clients. I wish I had taken this approach years ago. It is just a really exciting time to be in this business. Well enough about me. How about you Dorothy? What do you do? Oh really? How interesting, please tell me about that."

So, to dissect that suggested phraseology, you have just described an attractive situation that any reasonable person would want to be a part of, but you made no overtures to doing business together. You alluded to your approach by talking about the great relationships you have formed, which displays your integrity. You also projected great scarcity for yourself, and, in the process, you have made yourself attractive. Anyone reading between the lines sees someone who clearly does not need the business, and your probing questions about them show charm and confidence.

I know of a young advisor that uses this exact approach. He worked previously at one of the 'Baby Bell' telecom companies and continued to network with his past colleagues and some other local groups. In seven months he had seven clients that all had three million or more each in investable assets. Those seven clients were by design. He had set an ideal client profile for himself that included a defining note stating his target market was people in the three-million-plus range in investable assets, and he stuck to it religiously.

This advisor had incredible discipline and word started to get around. Every time one of his ex-colleagues asked him what he was doing these days, he delivered his anti-elevator mantra, and then started gathering F.O.R.M. information on whoever he was talking to.

Because of his discipline, you can imagine it was only a matter of time before someone said: *"You know, I am not that satisfied with my advisor right now. Are you taking on new clients?"* He would reply: *"Well, that possibility is there for sure, but it has to be a good fit for me, and for you, of course. How about you give me your number, and I will call you when I am at the office. I have an initial meeting process I use that helps the two of us mutually determine whether or not we might be a good fit for each other."*

After this, they would get back to having fun, or business, or whatever they happened to be doing. It is an incredibly disarming approach, and unlike that which many have come to expect (and even dread) in these situations.

"I Just Lost a $7 Million Client?!"

One of the biggest benefits of a personal branding strategy is that it ensures your clients fully understand and appreciate the value you provide for them. That, in turn, helps insulate them from competitive factors. Yes, branding impacts client acquisition because your clients can describe you and articulate your value to someone else in a compelling way, but you also can't underestimate the importance of competitor-proofing.

The longer a relationship exists, the more familiar it becomes and the more things can be taken for granted and trivialized. This is especially true in an abstract and turbulent business that focuses on knowledge and intangibles. You have clients today who stay with you because they like and trust you in general terms, but that doesn't mean they are immune to the steady bombardment of promises made by the advisors trying to lure your clients away. These competitors are throwing the kitchen sink at your clients trying to instill that nagging feeling in their minds that there is a better asset management approach available than the one you are providing now.

It should go without saying that you can't take your clients for granted. But it's probably less obvious to you that you can't take it for granted that your clients are fully aware of all that you do in a clear and comprehensive way.

In speaking with successful advisors on a regular basis, I often hear stories about the shock that comes when a substantial, long-term client departs. Usually the advisor says to me, *"I don't understand why he would leave. I've made him a lot of money."*

I'll ask the advisor if there were any signs, to which the advisor will usually say that they never saw it coming. Often, when I follow up and ask the advisor to reflect on any changing patterns in the client's behavior prior to the departure, the response is different. With the benefit of hindsight, the advisor will recall a change in enthusiasm or recall some of the questions or comments the client made that seemed out of character. Reactions generally prompted by a competitor who got their foot in the door and crept onto the client's radar.

In some cases the advisor asked the departing client what happened, and why he or she felt compelled to move, to which the client replied with some variation of *"It was time for a change."* What that actually means is that there has been a lack of contact and communication, rather than poor execution or performance.

Often a client's reason for leaving will be vague. It could be that the former client was too polite to pin-point where the disconnect truly was. Then again, maybe it wasn't anything specific. In the minds of many clients a subtle apathy builds over time and they leave because they feel the relationship ran its course. It just naturally came to an end as far as they were concerned.

I can't over-stress that a durable relationship isn't just tied to the performance you achieve and the investment solutions you provide. There are several other pieces to the advocacy puzzle, many of which are value-added above and beyond what the client expects; but it's only value-added if it is something that the client understands. If your clients aren't aware of all the value you provide, they won't understand your value nor will they appreciate it. As a result, the more familiar the relationship becomes, without that clear understanding, the more you will be trivialized.

Building a real relationship, learning to listen and use that knowledge in your conversations with clients, differentiating yourself and ensuring clarity all keep you from falling victim to loyalty fatigue, and all of those factors are heavily influenced by your F.O.R.M. process.

Integrate F.O.R.M. with your Client Goal Setting Process

Of the many steps of the personal branding process that can fast-track clients to advocacy, and keep existing clients tied to you, this has to be among the easiest. When you onboard a new client or have a review meeting with an existing client, ensure that there is a tab in their Personal Financial Organizer (The PFO Binder that is the central hub of your relationship) that outlines the importance of F.O.R.M. Explain that you take a holistic and panoramic approach to client relationships and that part of your process is to know as much about your client's Family dynamics, Occupational issues and Recreational interests as you do about their Money. This dovetails with your trailer that we "shot" back in the first section.

Many clients will be amazed that you are so thorough and comprehensive. A few will wonder what the real benefits are. Either way, to drive the point home further, integrate F.O.R.M. with your client goal-setting process. Again, be panoramic and all-encompassing. You want to understand their financial goals, but you also want to understand what money means to them holistically as it relates to their family, occupation and recreational goals.

I recommend advisors develop and use a goal-setting process with clients and include that document in the F.O.R.M. tab within their PFO. This is a tangible and meaningful way to effectively make connections for the client as it relates to family investment legacy and transition issues, occupational retirement goals as well as business succession objectives, bucket lists, etc. - all of which become more predictable when tied into the solutions you provide. You can adapt the heart of theW5 Process to use as a framework for this goal-setting.

When you and your clients are crystal clear about all the reasons *why* they want to achieve financial independence, they place far more value on *how* you plan to get them to there. This will competitor-proof your clients in a way that ensures that anyone trying to steal them will meet resistance and dead ends with every effort. It's a win-win situation, because the more your now-competitor-proof client buys into your process and understands and appreciates it, the easier it will be for them to describe that process to someone else. You're more referable.

Many advisors tell me that their clients say that they 'don't talk about money with their friends and family members.' What they are actually saying is that they aren't clear about the advisor's process or how endorsing the advisor to someone else will ultimately reflect on them. Or, they are concerned that you will try to sell their acquaintance on buying an investment product and becoming a client. If that ever happens, use the misconception as an opportunity to re-frame their perception and start the process of helping them understand your commitment to stewardship rather than salesmanship. To accomplish that, say something like this (and you'll note a recurring theme):

"Fair enough. The reason I'm asking is because a major component of my value proposition is in making myself available to act as a sounding board for friends and family members of my clients. They do not need to become a client of mine to take advantage of this service. Especially when it comes to family members, because I have developed and refined a Family Investment Legacy Process for clients who are thinking about succession issues. So, no worries if this isn't relevant or something you are comfortable with. I just want my clients to be aware that I will make myself available to be a sounding board for people who are important to my clients. Frankly it's the most fulfilling aspect of my job and one of the primary reasons I became a professional advisor."

The above addresses the elephant in the room. Many people today mentally define a professional advisor as a broker asking them to buy something as opposed to a consultant asking them to buy into a process and long-term relationship. That's their expectation and you cannot feed it – you have to differentiate using effective messaging in all of your communication channels.

The Promise of Process

Let me sum up the interplay of branding and process that I have repeatedly touched on.

You want to be perceived as a consultant with a process as opposed to a salesperson with a quota, but you have to define yourself. Tell clients or prospective clients you have a process. Repeat it. Keep reminding them. If you don't define yourself, you will be defined automatically.

It's amazing how much trouble many top-caliber advisors have with this issue. Some advisors try so hard to make their value proposition unique that they end up reciting a long-winded elevator speech or mission statement that is, frankly, just a collection of words and sounds like everyone else. The goal isn't to create something earth shattering or esoteric, the goal is to create something simple and clear while instantly differentiating and elevating you.

When someone gives you the opportunity to explain your value proposition, I want you to ask yourself, *"what does this person really want?"* How you define yourself shouldn't address what you do in the literal sense, it should address what the person craves; a relationship with an expert who helps them achieve what they aspire to - financial independence and a greater sense of control.

By adding the phrase *"I have a process"*, you get their attention and you are instantly more attractive and compelling.

This goes beyond how a prospective client perceives you; it also addresses how an existing client describes you. Over time, through consistent communication, your clients will absorb this phraseology and weave it into their conversation when they have the opportunity to describe you to a friend or family member. Wouldn't it be great if a client shined a light on you by saying, *"You should talk to my advisor. I've never felt better about the track I'm on with my investments and, best of all, he has a process to ensure all the pieces of my financial puzzle are in place."* or *"I've had other advisors in the past that didn't even come close to the professionalism of my current advisor. She has a process to ensure that everything is addressed and her service is impeccable."*

That is just the beginning. A personal branding strategy helps people connect with you on a deeper level. The firm you represent has its own brand, but you need to build a brand within that brand. This adds credibility to your overall brand, but people are connecting with you, the messenger, not just your message in terms of solutions, products or rates of return.

You have to take your branding strategy beyond just the words you verbalize in a value proposition. It has to be integrated into all other forms of communication and every step of your process.

Don't Just Say You Have a Process, Show That You Have One

You must have a linked and sequential array of tools that people can hold in their hands to fully conceptualize and experience your approach. It is far more powerful to show someone your process than it is to just tell them you have one. Not only is it more impactful and memorable, but it also makes it much easier for the client to describe your value to someone else.

One vital example of this would be your fit process and new client onboard approach. I'll go into this in more detail, later, but here are three simple steps that you should always follow, each of which demonstrates you follow a process rather than just talk about doing so.

Step 1: After you have an initial phone conversation with a prospect who has been referred to you, it is essential to send them an introductory kit to build anticipation and predisposition before they've met you.

Step 2: When you meet with the prospect and exchange pleasantries, it is essential that you provide a printed agenda to demonstrate your professionalism.

Step 3: After the fit meeting leading up to the signing ceremony, you should then provide them with the welcome organizer to outline all of your services in a way that is positioned as a benefit to the client.

There are many other ways to enhance your branding strategy through process and I'll outline more in the following section. These strategies are proven to amplify your ability to competitor-proof clients, capture money in motion, maintain your fee-worthiness and improve your refer-ability.

Your actions really do speak louder than words.

Visit **www.TheAdvisorPlaybook.com** for access
to the Playbook Implementation Program

Section 4: Professionalize the Client Experience

Organizing Yourself and Your Clients

When it comes to leadership, people always follow character first, strategy second - General Norman Schwarzkopf

---

Vapor to Paper

Professionalizing every aspect of your business – from your agendas to your onboarding process to your office itself – and infusing each element with your brand, governed by replicable process, is the key to moving from the business running you, to you running the business.

As I said, if you're going to tell people you have a process, it helps to actually have one. You can't just tell them about it, either. You have to show it to them.

You are a knowledge-for-profit professional. Your knowledge is your livelihood. I've said it before but it's worth saying again. You aren't selling tangible things; you are promoting the promise of the future. When it comes to relationship management and client acquisition, it is essential that you take the abstract nature of your business and make it easier to conceptualize by providing people concrete things they can hold in their hands. In this section I'll go into detail on some specific processes you can use to accomplish this.

Think about it for a moment. Aside from a prospectus, product brochure or statement, your business has become extremely virtual and complex. As a result, the commoditization of your role has been amplified to the point that clients can trivialize your value and leadership and focus solely on ROI. This can undermine loyalty, expectation management, on-going empowerment and endorsements.

Adding tangible tools to your approach helps remind both your affluent clients and your prospective clients that there are two types of advisors - salespeople and consultants - and what the differences between the two are.

The five tools that follow are being used by our advisor coaching clients who are deploying the Pareto System with tremendous results.

Prospective Client Introductory Kit

When a client or strategic partner refers someone to you, an essential first step after an initial phone call is to courier an introductory kit to the prospective client.

I mentioned this step earlier, but let's expand on it a bit. This kit isn't a brochure, It's a professional folder containing an overview of your value proposition, integration process and philosophy, as well as any content you might have to present, like a white-paper or article that you have written.

This helps you develop a relationship before you've met the prospective client and prompts the person to begin contrasting you favorably to their current advisor - the advisor they are considering moving away from.

First Appointment Portfolio

When a prospective client meets you for the first time, they are feeling both anticipation and apprehension. After the pleasantries and as you segue to the formal part of the meeting, hand the prospective client a leather portfolio containing a notepad, pen and printed agenda. Watch the apprehension melt away as they realize you are a professional who uses an agenda - and who has no hidden agenda. They can take notes during your meeting and have a take-away to review as they work through your fit process. Again, the contrast and lasting impression helps them feel compelled to work with you.

PFO Welcome Binder

When you onboard a new client, explain to them that the asset management process is fluid and dynamic.

There are critical life events that occur that render any current financial plan obsolete. As a result, their needs will evolve as their life unfolds. This PFO binder is the hub that contains a menu of all of your services to future-pace the client. It raises the awareness that you can serve all of their unmet needs as they develop. The binder can hold their tax returns, will, estate planning documents and other key statements. This binder becomes the glue that galvanizes your relationship and serves as a springboard to their accountant, lawyer and other potential strategic partners.

Greeting Cards

Own the mantle whenever you pay tribute to a client using a greeting card. For a birthday, holiday, important milestone, referral thank-you, or to welcome a new client as part of your onboard process, send a card that has impact that stops them in their tracks when they open it, and lasting shelf-life to the point that they can't bring themselves to discard it.

Anchors

There are moments of truth that occur virtually every day that can define your relationship with a client. They reveal something about what is going on in their lives. They endorse you to a friend. They attend one of your events. Whatever the case may be, if you feel compelled to give your client a gift as a token of your appreciation, or as a simple gesture to display how you value the relationship, again ensure it has impact and shelf life.

Impact speaks to their interest based on what you know about them as revealed by your F.O.R.M. data. This is where listening plays such a role for the best of the best. A book about an interest or that addresses a personal issue is an example with both impact and shelf life. It speaks to them and it sticks around. For the wine-loving client who just referred a friend to you, a wine decanter has just as much impact as a bottle of wine, but far more shelf life.

Consultants focus on the lifetime value of a relationship. You are in the relationship business as much as you are in the field noted on your business card. Use tangible tools as a symbol of your professionalism and as an extension of your brand, and your results will be outstanding.

Speaking of tangible tools – how much thought have you given to your place of business?

The Multi-Sensory Office: Creating a Memorable, Refer-able Experience

When it comes to practice management, a lot of attention must be placed on the client experience. Using an agenda, having a fit process, onboarding a client systematically and deploying a service matrix are just a few of the essentials that I help advisors put into action to project professionalism and strengthen their client relationships. While all of those are essential, one of the most overlooked and trivialized components of the client experience is how your office, and the time your clients spend there, ultimately makes them feel about you.

I've had consultations over the years with top advisors who have shared some of the creative minor adjustments they've made to their office environments; changes that have led to major improvements in terms of client feedback, loyalty, empowerment and refer-ability.

The office experience you create is an extension of your personal branding. It helps clients connect with you on a deeper level. Consistent service, expectation management and performance will always be primary factors when it comes to long-term relationships, but there are many other factors you can utilize to help insulate your relationships from the things outside your control. How clients feel about you, especially when they meet with you in your office, contributes to their sense of belonging, which can contribute greatly to refer-ability. I can also tell you this: Many advisors have told me that their clients mention how much they love their advisor's office environment and team culture when they are describing that advisor to a friend.

Your Waiting Area

Think of your top 20 clients. Have you identified any commonalities in terms of their interests? They reveal F.O.R.M. information to you over time, so ensure that you have five or ten relevant and current magazines neatly displayed that they can peruse in the ten minutes they may wait for you when they arrive. Large coffee table books covering the same interests (common examples being wine, cooking, travel, art, music or dogs) and other topics should be available, too.

That is just the start. Do you serve an array of top quality beverages to your clients? Do you know what their preferences are (stemming from their F.O.R.M. profile) in advance of their arrival, and is it ready for them? Perhaps a photo album with pictures of the events, charitable causes, and local athletes you sponsor?

Make the Initial Impression a Memorable One

Several advisors have told me that, in addition to a well-stocked beverage fridge, additional great investments they've made include a quality cappuccino machine and small pastry oven. Freshly made croissants, cookies and coffee create a nice aroma, and staff members look forward to showing off their preparation skills.

Others, who prefer to keep it simple yet still tap into the world of aroma therapy, go to Tommy Bahama or a bath-and-body store to ensure the scent in the office is pleasant. One advisor told me that his staff changes the scent seasonally - pine in Q4, the tropics in Q1, floral in Q2, and a summer scent in Q3.

The key here is subtlety and understatement. Scents can be over the top and come on too strongly, so you want to find an appropriate level.

The Restroom

Or, as we call it in Canada, the washroom, should be immaculate on all levels. This isn't always possible if you have common facilities in your office space, but I can tell you that many advisors inform me that they spare no expense to ensure the visit to that room is a positive experience. Make a statement with the quality of supplies, the tasteful approach to décor, and it will be appreciated. The bar has been lowered to such a degree over the years that it's not that hard to stand out. Ensure your team is empowered to make the effort, especially in this area.

Your Meeting Room

If you have a separate meeting room in addition to your own office, I encourage you to create a den-like atmosphere that is subtle and understated, yet warm and comfortable.

I've convinced many advisors who were going to spend heavily to renovate and modernize their rented office space to instead acquire quality vintage furnishings, actual art instead of bland wall-decor, area rugs and lamps to create a nicer vibe. Rather than spending the money on leasehold improvements and boring corporate furniture, they instead acquired tasteful assets that belong to them, hold their value, are portable and add far more character and personality to the office environment.

Many advisors have run with this and have acquired office decor, accent pieces, and artwork from the various countries they've traveled to in order to spark conversations with clients about what they ultimately want to use their investment income for: New life experiences and accomplishments. Where possible, include items that echo or imply your process and your branding.

Your Personal Office

I've been in countless offices of professional advisors over the years. The ones that stand out the most are those that reflect the interests and passions of the advisor and create an ambiance that says "I am enjoying my life and I love coming to work."

Many advisors' offices lack personality and warmth, and clients pick up on the blandness, even if subconsciously. Again, you're not trying to impress people, you are just trying to impress upon them that your sense of purpose, your personal legacy and your overall fulfillment in life is being achieved.

If you've ever walked in to a spa, you already know they attempt to put you into a different state of mind the moment you pass through the doors. The music, the aroma, the flowers and textures are all in place to change your mindset and create a calm, serene and memorable experience. They want you to tune out the world and slow life down so that you can savor the moment.

What kind of experience do your clients have when they walk through your doors? You've been walking through those doors for years - sometimes in a trance - and you might be oblivious to the energy and impression it creates. Try to see it through the client's eyes and experience how their senses are impacted, and you will subtly strengthen your relationships even further. You and your team might even enjoy the environment a little.

Don't forget some wall décor that reinforces your branding symbol (your Nike Swoosh): An image of a swan, a bridge, a lighthouse or a pathway, for example. It's something that you can point to in order to take your value from abstract to understood.

The Not-So-Hidden Agenda

Let's create a scenario. You've been introduced to a prospective client. You have reached out and had an initial phone call. After the call you sent your introductory kit by two-day courier and now you're about to meet the prospective client for an initial appointment.

I'm going to let you in on a little secret and expand into more depth on casting yourself in the all-important stewardship role.

Many of the most successful professional advisors I know have increased their persuasive impact by radically altering their sales process with prospective clients. These advisors (many of whom used to be salespeople) have evolved into professional consultants; they now strive to attract new clients rather than chase them. Instead of using the old-school sales process to close business, they use a fit process to fast-track new clients to advocacy.

When I consult with an advisor as part of our gap analysis process, one of the first things I'll do is scrutinize the approach he or she uses for prospective client meetings. I then ask these two questions:

Who views it as an accomplishment when you bring on a new client? Are you celebrating because you've closed them or are they excited because they've qualified to work with you?

Do you ask clients to buy from you or do you ask them to buy into a relationship with you?

For many advisors, nowhere in their onboarding process does a new client need to convince the advisor that there is a good fit. It's the advisor doing all the convincing and, in the process, their salesmanship is actually undermining the lifetime value of the relationship.

When you sell to someone, there is often a sense of anticlimax for the new client and perhaps a chance that they are feeling some degree of buyer's remorse. The advisor cannot be the only one who gets excited when a new relationship is formed. The client has to have a sense of accomplishment, too. This is one reason that I suggest turning your prospective client process upside down.

Instead of pushing prospective clients into making a decision, you can engage and then empower them. Our time-tested, up-front approach has been proven to attract new clients. It combines the use of an agenda with a process that highlights the importance of a relationship based on fit rather than one based on pressure and urgency.

When a prospective client approaches your office for the first time two emotions are front and center: Anticipation and apprehension. The anticipation stems from the person's curiosity about you. It is possible, for example, that the prospective client is meeting with you because someone spoke highly of you and recommended your services. Keep in mind that every prospective client you meet already has a professional advisor, and is probably meeting with you because he or she is to some degree disillusioned with that relationship. As a result, the prospect is seeking an alternative.

At the same time, the prospective client is apprehensive, fearing change, fearing the unknown and fearing the expected "sales pitch". People are sold to each and every day. Consequently, they put up walls when they are in a selling encounter. It's a natural self-defense mechanism.

Don't Meet Their Expectations

Most prospective clients walk into a meeting bracing for a presentation in which you strongly promote your products and services. If they assume that your ultimate goal - your hidden agenda - is to sell them something, why feed that expectation? Instead, you can do something completely unexpected.

When you meet with a prospective client, shake hands, exchange pleasantries, then sit down and slide a leather portfolio that includes a note pad and pen as well as a printed agenda across the table for him or her to examine. Then launch into the formal segment of the meeting with a personalized version of this opening statement:

"Mr./Mrs. Prospective Client, let me begin by saying how much I appreciate you taking the time to be here today. I know your time is valuable and my goal is to ensure that you feel this meeting was a wise investment. Now, I know you are here primarily to assess my professional credentials and approach, and to get to know more about my firm. I will share this information with you during this initial meeting. I wanted to meet with you to get to know you and to determine if we will have good chemistry over the lifetime of our potential relationship. This is a step in my overall process. Therefore, because a relationship like this is important for both of us, no one will be making any commitments today. At the end of our meeting, as part of my process, I'll be getting together with my team to discuss your situation, and we'll discuss our compatibility. I'll then call you in 48 hours to let you know if we think we'd be a good fit for you. You can take some time to decide if there is a fit as well. Is that fair?"

A statement like this is a refreshing departure from the usual s
of a first meeting, and it has positive results. You will immediat
prospective client's body language change. Tension and appreh
melt away when he or she realizes that this is not a typical selling
The prospect was probably expecting the usual pitch process, where the
meeting builds to the point at which they are asked to buy a service. Imagine
how much better your potential client will feel when you instead highlight
the importance of "buying into" a meaningful relationship. You will instantly
disarm and impress.

To come back to the introduction portfolio, this leather folder is a
powerful and tangible tool that they can hold and take away with them. It
anchors them to your professionalism. Using an agenda at these meetings is
important. It instantly gives the prospective client a tangible track to follow
and it eliminates any fear that you will introduce unwelcome surprises. An
agenda is simply an outline with talking points, with the prospective client's
name on the top and a series of bullets which highlight the main topics that
you will discuss at the meeting, things like:

1st Mtg. Agenda

- **Getting to Know Each Other**
- **An Introduction to My Firm**
- **An Overview of My Philosophy, Planning Strategy and Process**
- **What's Important to You?**
- **My Value-Added Services**
- **Is There a Fit?**

The agenda gives the client a feeling of certainty. It also benefits you
because it establishes where the meeting will go next, so you can actually
listen to the prospective client. The agenda makes it easy for you to explain
some of the your more abstract professional concepts because it provides
specific talking points. Again, you are in the knowledge-for-profit business.
You aren't selling something tangible; you are promoting the promise of a
comfortable future insulated from external circumstances. You need all the
help you can get to demystify what it is that you do.

After all, it's not what you say that matters, it's what the prospective client
hears and internalizes.

Often, when asking an affluent prospect about their relationship with their current professional, a typical response is that "all is well" and that "everything is just fine". Unfortunately, these prospects don't know what they don't know, and we have found it a best practice of the elite professional to help draw a contrast between the experience they are currently receiving and the potential of something much greater.

Allow me to share with you the dialog of contrast to expose the incumbent. I would first tell you what not to do, however:

Never attack the incumbent provider

Never attack the incumbent firm

A sure-fire way of turning a prospect into a defendant is to attack a decision that they have made. A clear decision that we can agree isn't in the best interest of the prospect is to be working with someone other than *you*. Nevertheless, if we default into pointing out all the "wrong" that the other professional is doing, or black the eye of the incumbent firm, it is the decision of our prospect that we are calling into question. Instead, allow the prospect to arrive at their own conclusion.

When positioning what you do as superior to the incumbent, try to ask questions that assume the same level of service that you are delivering. For example, a conversation might run as follows:

Advisor: *I'm curious, when the advisor you are working with now comes out for their semi-annual face-to-face with you and your family, are you comfortable with how those meetings are going?*

Prospect: *We don't meet together that often.*

Advisor: *It's probably not that important, then.*

Prospect: *Well, I'm not saying that, we would like to have better and more frequent contact for sure.*

Advisor: *Interesting, we will come back to that.*

Or, to use another example:

Advisor: *I'm curious: When you do get together and they go over your PRA report with you - the two-page analysis that summarizes your retirement goals and tracks the likelihood of you reaching your retirement and legacy goals - are you comfortable with where your PRA number is?*

Client: *I've never even heard of that before. PRA?*

Advisor: *Interesting. We'll come back to that.*

Each of these examples communicates your experience and references your process. They evoke the contrast principle by casting yourself positively, rather than negatively commenting on an incumbent.

No, Really - Is There a Fit?

The most important bullet point on the agenda is the last one, which should always be "is there a fit?" When you get to this stage of the meeting, you thank the prospective client for attending, and remind him or her that you will now meet with your team. Confirm that you will contact him or her in 48 hours.

At this point, one of two things will happen. In some cases, the prospective client will thank you and tell you they look forward to hearing from you. More often than not, however, the prospective client will try to close *you*; they will try to convince you that *you* should take action right now.

I'm not making this up. Because of your forthright and disarming process, the prospective client will have developed a high degree of self-motivation and predisposition. He or she will likely say to you, "I don't need to think about it. I'm confident that there is a good fit and I'm prepared to move forward right now."

So how should you respond to this statement? I tell advisors to say this: *"Mr./Mrs. Prospective Client, I appreciate your enthusiasm. However, if that is how you feel, that won't change in 48 hours. This is important, so take your time. This is a process we like to follow so let me discuss it with my team."*

Ultimately, you live by the rules you set. If you cave in to the prospective client's request to move ahead immediately, then your entire meeting structure becomes nothing more than a tactic - a gimmick - and you seriously undermine your integrity.

There is only one situation in which I would suggest that you could make an exception. If a great client has referred the prospective client to you, and if the prospective client perfectly meets your Ideal Client criteria based on Assets, Attitude and Advocacy, you can consider making the exception. If you do so, be sure to make it clear that this *is* an exception. Otherwise, delay instant gratification and stick with the process.

This process empowers a prospective client to come to his or her own conclusions, and to feel great about coming on board with you. Furthermore, you are fast-tracking the process of turning a new client into an advocate who is competitor-proof and predisposed to referring other prospective clients to you.

When I conduct seminars on this topic, invariably there will be an advisor in the room who has worked with us in the past and has adopted our approach. Like clockwork, when I finish talking, the advisor will stand up and say, "He's right, this really works!" To that, I respond by saying, "It works because it's right."

Just One More Thing: The Columbo Close

Hopefully you are familiar with Peter Falk's great detective character Columbo. If not, you may want to add that to your "to watch" list. In any case, Columbo had a signature move in almost every interrogation. He would wrap up, excuse himself and start to leave, only to shrug in an aw-shucks way as though he'd forgotten something unimportant and turn back to the suspect (who had, of course, started to relax) to casually ask what was, usually, the case-breaking question.

Just before you let them go, while the client is relaxed and the "usual" pattern of sales has been broken, say just one more thing:

"Before I let you go, I just want to let you know that, as a value added service I provide for my clients that they really find to be beneficial, I make myself available to be a sounding board for their friends and family members. Should we find we're a fit and decide to work together, I will outline that process for you."

It plants a seed, as well as helping cement your value and your consciousness of the things that matter to them. You can point back to this when you onboard the client, too.

The Onboarding Process: How to Fast-Track a New Client to Advocacy

My favorite stories stem from conversations I have with our coaching team who share success stories from the field with me. Our team and I often have "Proof that it Works" conversations where they pass along feedback in terms of the impact our strategies are having on an advisor's business.

Recently, I heard an interesting example about the importance of the New Client Process. This process is the series of steps that take place from the moment you get a referral phone call right up to the point where you officially welcome a new person as a client.

At a glance, the New Client Process has five distinct parts. In the previous section, we've looked in detail at the first two:

- **The Pre-Appointment Phase**
- **The First Appointment (or Fit Appointment)**
- **The Second Appointment**
- **The Third Appointment (if needed, depending on a client's sophistication)**
- **The New Client Welcome**

Some might say that this seems like a lot of steps, but these are all necessary steps. This process is extremely attractive to potential clients, and more often than not, as a result of going through this process, the potential client ends up trying to convince the advisor to take them on as a client. I also see advisors get referrals from someone shortly after bringing them on as a client. I see it happen all the time.

The coach who shared the following story with me worked with two brothers who have a successful practice in California. Both use this New Client Process, and they are enjoying a lot of success from this process and from their terrific implementation of it.

One of the brothers recently met with a prospective client, a wealthy lady who had more than $1,000,000 in investable assets. As they sat down, and as the advisor pulled out the agenda to start the meeting, the lady said, "I want you to know that I am interviewing different advisors."

The advisor, in a cool and collected way, replied, "Well, I would be surprised if you weren't. The reality is that we are interviewing you today as well. It is very important to our practice that my brother and I only take on clients that are a good fit."

I wish that I had been in the room when they were having this meeting, so I could have seen how the dynamic changed after the advisor replied in this fashion. He didn't try to sell harder or any of that nonsense, he just stated the truth, which was that there were two decisions being made that day, both hers and his.

The wealthy lady became a client. It turned out that she had interviewed four different advisors in total, and the third such interview was with our client. It was just a few days later when a thank-you card arrived at the advisor's office. It was from the same lady, and in the card she thanked them for deciding to take her on as a client. What a change in attitude from that first meeting, and it all had to do with the attractiveness of the New Client Process, and the skill of our client in implementing it.

The woman wasn't done yet though. Shortly after the thank-you card arrived, my client received an email from her. She had copied her CPA on the email, and the message said: "You guys have to meet each other". The advisor gave the CPA a call, and they got together for lunch.

Over lunch, my client learned that the CPA had a huge operation with 24 staff, and they specialized in ultra-high-net-worth types; the richest of the rich.

The advisor and his brother specialize in clientele in the $1-10 million range. The advisor candidly told the CPA this, and also told him that the ultra-high-net-worth types weren't really their niche.

It turns out that the $1-10 million range wasn't the CPA's niche either. His focus was going to remain on the ultra-high-net-worth types, and he and the advisors are now discussing the CPA referring over business in the $1-10 million range to them as it appears. He regularly receives those types of referrals, but isn't really interested in that kind of business. The advisors certainly are, though!

Their next step is to show the CPA the highlights of the New Client Process, so that when the CPA does refer someone, he can have great confidence that they will be well looked after, and how that process will roll out.

The bottom line is this: When you apply stewardship over salesmanship with a prospective client, you not only contrast yourself favorably to other advisors, you are also positioning yourself for advocacy with that person, immediately.

Document Your Onboarding Process

Let's go back to our scenario. Your initial meeting has gone well. You've established there's a fit with that prospective client. Now you want to onboard and fast-track this person to advocate status.

One of the most important procedures you can document and refine is that of onboarding new clients. The benefits of starting a new relationship professionally include:

Validation - The new client was probably referred from an existing client or strategic partner. At some point in the future these two people are going to connect and you want the new client to say "Thank you for introducing me to your advisor". That validation makes you more referable and increases the likelihood that the referrer will do it again.

Contrast - The new client will contrast your client experience to that of their former advisor. Positive contrast solidifies their decision and competitor-proofs them in the future.

Self-motivation – The new client feels so good about their decision that they feel compelled to wave your flag to others. They know how to describe you because the experience is positive, clear and fresh in their minds.

In our Pareto System program, the entire new client experience consists of 21 sequential steps. This includes the process of connecting with a prospective client, establishing a fit and bringing them on as a client. In this section, I'd like to outline the onboarding portion of the process. It consists of four simple steps:

1. **Sending a Thank You Card**
2. **Sending a Team-Client Service Letter**
3. **Sending a Client Binder to keep things organized**
4. **Making a first statement review call**

The defining features of a good thank-you card are two-fold. You want it to have impact and you want it to have shelf life. To achieve that, send out the nicest card you can find, as I talked about earlier. Be certain to use the proper phraseology too. Don't say "Thanks for the business" in your card. Downplay the productivity and play up the relationship. Instead, make an observation about something the client revealed in the conversation.

"I really enjoyed meeting with you today and I'm looking forward to a great relationship. I loved hearing about your recent trip to the Napa Valley. I'll have to pick your brain soon about your favorite wineries. Cheers and welcome aboard!"

You want to pay tribute to the commitment to a relationship rather than the commission you will earn.

The Big Picture

About a week after the signing ceremony, send the new client a formal letter introducing your team and their specific roles while restating your commitment to client service. *"We take a team approach and I'd like to introduce you to our staff, outline their roles and provide their direct phone numbers."*

The Even Bigger Picture

About two weeks after the signing ceremony, send out the PFO leather binder to the client. You'll want to show it to them when they first become a client.

"We take great pride in keeping our clients organized. We'll be sending this binder to you in a couple of weeks once we get it organized for you. Be sure to put everything you receive from us in here and bring this with you to review meetings."

Explain that there are multiple pieces to the financial puzzle and, as the client's life unfolds, their needs will evolve. Include a list of all your services to plant the seed that you are their personal CFO. This way, in review meetings you can "future pace" your clients to ensure that they always contact you as new needs present themselves. This binder becomes an important symbol they can hold in their hands. It galvanizes your value not just now, but in the future as well. This has proven to be the best way to harness money in motion.

Lock Down

About 45 days after the signing ceremony, and as part of the process of initiating a proactive call rotation with your new client, you or a team member can touch base to conduct a First Statement Review Call. Chances are you'll just leave a voice mail stating, *"I just wanted to check in with you. You will have received your first statement from us and we want to make sure that you can clearly understand everything."*

This new client will have probably received more value in the first two months of your relationship than in the last 12 months of their prior professional advisor relationship. This process will validate that they did the right thing in moving to you, contrast you favorably and propel them to become a self-motivated advocate quickly and predictably.

It's one thing to want referrals. It's another thing to deserve them. Ask yourself if the service you provide is enough to consider yourself referable – something we'll go into in much greater depth. A commitment to consistent best practices is the foundation of advocacy which leads to fully maximized relationships instead of just a client base.

Mistaking Motion for Action

Let me return to Hemingway's phrase and look at the difference between being active and merely moving. When I ask a professional advisor, "How are things?" nine times out of ten, the answer will be, "I'm extremely busy." Our response is always, "Busy doing what?"

The *Law of Cause and Effect* states that your activities will determine your productivity. If you want your productivity to increase, the first place you should look is the activities you engage in which give you the best return on your investment of time and energy.

Think about it. The Pareto Principle states that 80 percent of your productivity stems from about 20 percent of your activities. In other words, you make about 80 percent of your income every day in one golden hour. What goes into that hour? Talking to and meeting with your favorite clients and the most predisposed prospective clients available to you. All other activities must support these two essential activities.

Unless you are a one-person operation, one of the most obvious ways to increase your capacity to do more of what you get paid to do is to delegate as many supporting activities as possible. You either have an assistant, or you are one.

For many entrepreneurs, managing people and the accompanying hassles can be a big issue. Many perceive staff management as actually exacerbating the problem because it can be a distraction. Hiring new people adds yet another expense and could potentially upset the chemistry of the staff currently in place.

These concerns can be addressed if you step back and scrutinize your business. Determine whether it is truly built on predictable, sustainable and duplicable systems driven by accountability and consistency. Does everyone on your team know their job description? Do they follow predetermined systems and procedures, or are they left to their own devices?

I have seen many entrepreneurs with successful businesses supported by talented people who unknowingly created self-imposed limitations because everyone in the organization flew by the seat of their pants. Time after time, the creation of an Organizational and Structural Chart followed by the refinement of systems outlined within a Procedures Manual has proven to be essential.

Systems Create Success

A major step toward professionalizing and depersonalizing your business is to craft an Organizational Chart. It is a snapshot of everyone on your team with a brief description of what they do. One sheet of paper is required and, when completed, it becomes the cover sheet of your Procedures Manual.

If you have never done this before you may be wondering if it is worth the effort. Time and time again, when conducting a gap analysis for one of our coaching and consulting clients, we have determined that in order to develop a systematized business this is an essential "step back" in order to take several steps forward.

The *Random House Dictionary* defines 'system' as "a group or combination of things or parts forming a complex or unified whole." Does this sound like your business? Dry as it may be, it fits the reality that is critical for your success.

Take a hard look at your operation. Would it run like a Swiss watch if you weren't there all the time? Could you convince me, today, that your enterprise is a true business and not just a company that sells things? Have you created something with great value, predictable outcomes and ironclad systems? Could you provide documentation detailing exactly how to operate and run your business right down to the smallest detail?

If you have created a business with true systems, you already know the freedom and control it has brought to your business and personal life. The haphazard approach cannot compare

So where do you start? If you are going to build a business based on systems, the first step is to clearly define each individual's responsibilities within your organization. You and your team have to sit down and determine who does what and when.

On a daily basis, you and your team engage in proactive and reactive activities. Based on the *Law of Cause and Effect*, all of these activities affect your productivity. You and your team need absolute clarity on who is accountable for each of these activities to ensure processes carry through consistently.

Do the Monkeys Run the Zoo?

Not to compare your team to monkeys, but process and role-setting has a huge impact on establishing productivity. If you have kids, you know that clear boundaries have to be established, rules of engagement and codes of conduct have be reinforced constantly and, ultimately, you have to lead by example. Otherwise they will unconsciously drift and test the limits to push beyond what you've established.

Don't misinterpret what I'm saying here, but when it comes to guarding your time and ensuring everyone values it fully, being productive and making the most of your capacity, you have to train your clients and your team.

Your clients have to know that you don't have a red phone under a glass jar sitting on your desk. If they need something urgently, they can reach your team members instantly – their phones and email are the Bat-Line – but not yours. You have a process and that's how you interact with them, with consistency.

Be forthright with your clients and team members by telling them that you set aside a window of time to reactively respond to phone messages and emails that are not urgent. Make it client-centered. Tell them this disciple ensures that you can consistently and pro-actively drive your roles and responsibilities as part of the professional client experience you're providing.

Interruptions can disrupt your focus. So don't allow them. Your team will respond instantly to the things that aren't major so that you don't end up reactively majoring in minor things. Some advisors feel the need to be accessible at all times. It's a dangerous pattern to fall into because, ultimately, it won't be as appreciated as you might think, and the perception of the value of your time will diminish. You live by the rules and processes you set, but unless you respect your time, your clients won't.

A mutually respectful relationship will survive volatility and thrive over the long haul.

Clients Should Be Loyal To a Process, Not Just To a Person

Stephen Covey, the legendary author of the book *The 7 Habits of Highly Effective People,* advised that you should always begin with the end in mind. It is for that reason I suggest that you apply a mindset of building a business with the intention of selling it for maximum value at some point in the future.

Even if the thought of selling your business hasn't crept into your mind, or is a distant vision for many years down the road, it's a good idea to apply the philosophy of maximizing the equity value in your business on an ongoing basis.

This goes beyond just practice management in the traditional sense. Deploying best-practices creates a client experience that generates loyalty and refer-ability, but if you don't document those procedures you are still only trading your time for money. You have a job that ultimately generates an hourly income for you. You can earn a tremendous living that way but you still want to keep an eye on the prize; maximizing the equity value of your business beyond just the Trailing Twelve Months.

The best business is one that earns you a living *and* builds your legacy. This dual track stems from creating and deploying predictable, sustainable and duplicable procedures that are documented in a playbook and are consistently implemented. This creates the consistency that your clients crave, which insulates them from competitive factors and other issues beyond your control, but the double-win is that, when it eventually comes time to sell your business, the suitor realizes your clients are loyal to your process and not just to you and the performance you generate.

Additionally, they realize that your procedures have not only created a durable business, they can also apply your procedures to their existing business. One plus one can equal three.

When it comes to maximizing the value of a business, the buyer wants to ensure continuity through and beyond the acquisition process. When all of your processes are documented in your playbook, and you present a transitional process to professionally communicate with clients well in advance of the transition, predictability elevates. This applies even if you plan to sell just a portion of your business through a right-sizing process.

The Rule of Three

Every action you perform three or more times, or which has three or more steps in the process, should be documented in your playbook. That is the *Rule of Three.*

Get everything out of your head and the heads of your team members. The benefits of a playbook go beyond just consistency and continuity. The efforts compound over time creating momentum - regardless of who is deploying them. If a business is driven by maverick talent who operate daily out of their heads, the value is lower than a business driven by the procedures contained in a playbook. The faces on your team may change over time but your processes remain.

That's not to say that you will always remain on auto pilot after you create a playbook. The *Law of Optimization* must be continuously applied to your business. When I ask an advisor *"Why do you do things that way?"* The answer is often the same: *"That's the way we've always done it."* They unconsciously drifted into a pattern and then arrived at a set-it-and-forget-it mode.

Einstein was right when he defined insanity as being the repetition of an action over time and expecting a different outcome. This explains why many knowledge-for-profit professionals who have been in the business for 15 years have one year of experience 15 times. They are making a living, but they aren't building a business that is valued for more than the industry average.

Make Yourself Obsolete

Earlier, I asked what would happen if you took a month off tomorrow; would your business run like a Swiss watch, or would there be chaos?

One advisor summed up the responses of many professionals quite well: "The only thing scarier than me taking a month off would be if my assistant took a month off. I don't really even know what she does fully, but my clients love her."

There is a big difference between having a job and building a business. With a job, you can earn money but you aren't building anything. You are trading your time for money. Building a business means that you can earn an income *and* build an asset. In other words, rather than just earning money, you can be worth a lot of money.

So, how do you build? Make your processes *yours.*

Get Your Business Out of Your Head

When you went through the W-5 process, what goals were established? Are you hoping to sell your business at some point down the road? If so, are you hoping that the value of your business won't be based solely on your trailing 12, as I touched on? Are you perhaps hoping that you can start taking more time off so that you can pursue other interests? You've given a lot to your business over the years, isn't it time it gave a little more back to you? Or perhaps you are thinking about expanding your business by bringing on a protégé or two so that you can leverage your skills a bit?

Whatever your goals are, if you want your business to serve your life rather than the other way around, you have to get your business out of your head (and your assistant's head) and start documenting your procedures. I know it sounds like work, but the payoff can be massive.

Turn Your Processes into Intellectual Properties

There is brilliant entrepreneurial maxim from *The E-Myth* that states that "You must work *on* your business, not just *in* your business." This means you must document your processes in order to refine and standardize them. This ensures that you create consistency in terms of how they are delivered to your clients and that nothing slips through the cracks. It also ensures that you are never at the mercy of maverick talent. In other words, if a staff member leaves you, your ability to train someone new and not miss a beat is predictable.

You and your team are probably all very competent, but you can always raise the bar. As I covered in the *Rule of Three*, any process that you execute more than three times and has more than three steps must be documented in order to find areas for improvement for consistent deployment. As an example, take your Client Onboarding Process. How many steps are there in your current process? Let's briefly revisit the five I talked about:

1. **A client calls to introduce you to a friend**
2. **You contact the friend a send out your introductory kit**
3. **You meet the prospect initially to help determine if there is a fit**
4. **You meet again for the signing ceremony**
5. **You onboard the client and start to fast-track him or her to advocate status**

Do you remember the 21 steps I mentioned that occur in the Pareto Systems version of that process? Based on the 80/20 Rule, the advisor deploys four of the steps and the assistant deploys the other 17. If the assistant is away, injured, on vacation, on maternity leave or has departed entirely, the new assistant could easily follow the process with precision. That is just one example, but you get my point.

There are a multitude of benefits that come from creating a playbook and documenting your processes. You convert your business procedures into valuable intellectual properties and, in the process, increase the value of your business. A book of business limited to assets on paper has a smaller value than an actual business with predictable, sustainable and duplicable systems. Furthermore, because of the consistent commitment to best practices, your ability to competitor-proof clients, uncover money in motion and be more referable become inevitable.

Let's not forget that Stuff Happens! If you need to switch firms or take an extended leave for medical or other personal reasons, your systems and procedures insulate you from many external pressure and dependencies. Risk management and scenario planning prepare you for the unexpected.

Lastly, when you start running the business instead of it running you, you restore liberation and order to your life. That takes ROI to an entirely new level, because not only does your income and the value of your asset grow, so too does the fulfillment that comes from owning an efficient business.

Moments of Truth: Events that Can Define Your Client Relationships

So now you have a new client. You want to competitor-proof this relationship, capture money in motion, to gain their full empowerment and earn their endorsements, and you do that through impeccable service.

By "service" I mean both reactive and proactive models. We'll talk more about proactive service using a service matrix but, for now, let's talk about reactive service, especially **Moments of Truth**. Moments of Truth occur when a client reveals something that's going on in their life.

You are a leader, and that leadership is something you'll want to express and use in reaction to Moments of Truth, so let's examine it.

You lead your clients through market turbulence and help them tune out the noise while staying focused on a plan and process. Without trivializing the importance of providing a solid investment strategy for your clients, your character and your ability to manage a relationship is just as important as your ability to manage a portfolio.

Think of it this way. The products and services you provide and the firm you represent are all part of your message. You are the messenger. When a prospective client meets you for the first time, they're connecting with the messenger before they buy into the message. When a client brags about you to a friend, they normally spend more time talking about the messenger. Ironically, many advisors spend most of their time promoting only the message.

The message isn't proprietary and much of it can be abstract to the client. It is also at the mercy of many external dependencies. I'm asking you to look at ways that you can complement the message by connecting with your clients on a deeper, more creative level. In the process you will make yourself indispensable to them, not to mention more referable. This approach is essentially an extension of your client service process and helps demonstrate your value to them.

There are many ways to do this that are either proactive or reactive. Proactive service consists of actions that can be automated and built into your on-going service matrix. Sending a birthday card every year to your clients, providing a welcome binder as part of your onboard process and using agendas in review meetings, are just a few of the many examples that can help you stand out, get people's attention and be memorable.

Reactive service, on the other hand, speaks to how you respond to *unique events*.

Moments of Truth are unique or rare events that take place between you and a client where they are saying "I trust you." They might bare their soul to you and reveal a challenge or setback they are experiencing. They might refer someone to you for the first time. Perhaps the client achieves an important personal milestone or accomplishment and decides to share it with you.

Just becoming a client is a Moment of Truth. Let's face it, they are leaving a relationship and selecting you. It's a big deal, and how you pay tribute and respond to it is important. Here are a few examples:

Your Client Reveals a Setback they are Experiencing

Chances are you've had a client who told you about some bad news they received, or an unpleasant event they were going through. Occasionally the news can be severe. I remember telling an advisor to send a client going through a tough patch a book called *When Bad Things Happen to Good People*. The advisor sent the book, along with a card with a thoughtful comment. A few days later the client called saying that the gesture was the most thoughtful thing anybody had done during that difficult period.

Your Client Reveals a Personal or Family Accomplishment

An advisor told me about a conversation with an affluent client who revealed that his son had finally, after several stops and starts, graduated from college. I suggested that the advisor send the son - a future client, ideally - a copy of the book *The Richest Man in Babylon* along with a card congratulating him on his success. A few days later, the dad called the advisor thanking him profusely for getting his son thinking about his own financial future.

Your Client Refers a Friend to You for the First Time

Another advisor told me about a very affluent client that had just sent his first referral in their seven-year relationship. The advisor asked me how he should say thank you. I asked him to tell me about the client.

After a brief description of interests the advisor mentioned that client had just purchased a motor home so that he and his wife could travel North America to visit friends and family while playing some of the more famous golf courses. I suggested that the advisor send a thank-you card as well as a subscription to *RV World Magazine*. The cost would be about the same as box of golf balls but the impact and shelf life would be far greater.

Again, I'm not suggesting you get into the gift-giving business, but when a moment of truth presents itself, it is important to be thoughtful and creative. When a client tells you something that goes beyond the superficial, or when a client takes action to your benefit, they are saying "I trust you." How you respond to such Moments of Truth can take your relationship to the next level and ensure the goodwill continues.

It comes down to expectations and contrast.

Your client wasn't expecting you to respond with as much impact as you did. It therefore stands out in their mind and galvanizes your relationship. They have a frame of reference in terms of how they expect a professional advisor to conduct himself or herself. Their former advisor didn't have a mindset of reactive service when it came to moments of truth. Therefore, your actions validate their decision to move over to you, and activate their conversion from client to advocate, and that is where the value is in this business; not in how many clients you have, but in how many *advocates* you have.

From M.O.R.F to F.O.R.M

One of the most important procedures you can put in place is a habitual approach to capturing F.O.R.M. information, and you need your team to buy into this process.

If you are like most professional advisors I work with, you place a tremendous importance on continually refining your wealth management acumen. You invest hundreds of hours each year into analyzing market trends, scrutinizing commentary from various gurus and researching countless investment vehicles and opportunities.

The benefits of this ongoing market study are two-fold. First, your continual commitment to self-improvement helps you meet your CE requirements. Second, you get to relay your findings to your clients to reinforce your value to them. This is where it gets interesting.

Not all clients are the same and you can't treat all clients the same way. About 20 percent of your clients are more demanding when it comes to conversations about all things related to money. They look at the M in F.O.R.M. first, usually Occupation and then Recreation and Family. In a typical conversation with these clients, it's down to business with just a few minutes dedicated to occupation, recreation and family. They're wired for M.O.R.F.

For these clients everything unrelated to money is an afterthought and a courtesy component in the conversation. Not to say these clients are bad, but they are the clients who are most likely to view you as a commodity, and are quickest to leave in an attempt to find "better numbers".

The chances are that the other 80 percent of your clients don't want to hear everything you know about money. They hire you to deal with that so they don't have to.

I am not trivializing the importance of bringing value to your clients' money. It is ultimately why they work with you, but bringing value to their money is a given. It's expected that you do a good job in your professional core skills. If all you do is what is expected, you will never stand out in your clients' minds and be memorable. You will be, for the most part, a commodity. You can imagine the impact this will have on your refer-ability. When you look for ways to exceed expectations and stand out in your clients' minds you galvanize relationships.

Moments of Truth, as I talked about earlier, occur in your conversations with clients and they can often define your relationships *if* you respond in a meaningful way. Often a client will reveal something of importance that is occurring in their life regarding their family, occupation or recreational interests.

Case in point, one of our coaches was speaking to an advisor client of ours who revealed that one of his high net-worth clients has a substantial family gathering each year around the 4th of July. This event is effectively their family Thanksgiving get-together because it is the only holiday they all can be in the same place at the same time.

During this gathering, there is a sporting tournament that everyone participates in. The winning team has bragging rights throughout the year. The advisor, thinking about the importance of family in the F.O.R.M. process, created a beautiful trophy with the family name and tournament title that would be presented to the winning team to be kept until next year's event. The impact this trophy had, not to mention the shelf-life, was colossal. The ROI was ridiculous.

Look for moments of truth that present themselves in your client relationships. When a client reveals something of importance to you about their family, occupation or recreational interests they are essentially saying "I trust you and value our relationship." When you respond in a meaningful way, you not only strengthen the chemistry you have together, you are also strengthening your personal brand and your refer-ability going forward.

So move your thinking from M.O.R.F. to F.O.R.M.

What is Your Capacity?

The one thing all professional advisors have an equal amount of is time.

We all have 24 hours in a given day. The concept of time-management is a bit of a misnomer. We can't manage time itself; we can only manage the activities we choose to engage in each business day. The more you value your time, the more your clients will, as well.

Of the many benefits that come from defining your process and procedures, your ability to project scarcity is high on the list. **The Law of Supply and Demand** says that if something is in scarce supply, the demand typically increases. What do you supply? Time! And you have to be unreasonable - both in terms of how it is allocated and the optics in terms of how it is valued.

I touched on this in the section *Do The Monkeys Run the Zoo,* but as a specific example: When was the last time you tried to get your dentist on the telephone? It just doesn't happen, does it?

Dentists are quite effective at guarding their time and creating rules of engagement that their clients respect. Let's face it, you don't want a tired, overworked, stressed-out or distracted dentist. You want someone who is relaxed and focused, and the most referable dentist is not just an effective dentist in terms of their *skill-set*; it's also their *mind-set* that is important. An attractive dentist is one who has managed to create an environment where you feel fortunate to be a client.

You aren't attracted to the dentist who has a sun-faded sign out front reading "Accepting New Patients". You are more inclined to gravitate to the dentist who is in such demand that their schedule won't allow a consultation for two months.

You feel accomplished because there is scarcity and value.

Work Half as Hard - Earn Twice as Much?

Since time is your limiting factor, you have to recognize that you don't have an unlimited capacity.

I'll never forget the first time the concept of client right-sizing occurred to me. An advisor was referred to us, and was inquiring about our coaching process. Within ten minutes, I learned that he had close to 900 clients, that he was making a ton of money and that he had no life.

He was stressed-out, out of shape and had a whole host of issues going on in his personal life. Clearly, the business was running him rather than the other way around. Then the advisor said, "I've heard good things about you. I'm thinking about hiring you to help me grow my business."

My reply to him was simple: "I think the best thing I can help you do is dismantle this thing."

My logic was that he had maxed-out and his growth and it was now starting to cost him more than it was getting him. It wasn't easy, and after some initial resistance, this advisor went from close to 900 clients down to about 200 clients. In short order, his stress and overhead went down while his productivity increased. Best of all, liberation and order were restored to his business and personal life.

Many elite advisors tell me that they have hit a plateau and they are having difficulties taking their businesses to the next level. In my experience, they hit this plateau because they still subscribe to the precept that you must continually "grow or perish." For a knowledge-for-profit professional, that is a fallacy. The maxim I suggest you live by is this: *Profit and progress, or perish.* You don't need to be bigger, you need to focus on getting better.

I want the assets you manage to grow year after year, but that does not mean that the number of relationships you manage must increase too. In fact, when it comes to relationships, the goal is not to see how big you can get, but rather how small you can stay.

Right sizing is often a critical step in moving to the next level. I can't begin to tell you how many advisors we've seen that have taken a proverbial step back in order to take a quantum leap forward. It's counter-intuitive, but over the past years, during the most severe head-wind this business has ever seen, this strategy has led many top advisors to a breakthrough.

Advisors who continually expand their client base eventually hit a point of diminishing returns. Once you exceed your service capacity, you can no longer effectively competitor-proof clients, gain their complete financial empowerment or maintain a high degree of refer-ability. As a result, you are likely to become stressed, frustrated and miss important opportunities. Furthermore, unless you hire and manage more staff, which takes time and money, you cannot effectively deploy your service matrix. In time, you will be perceived as a transactional generalist, and you will end up with a business that is a mile wide and an inch deep.

We come back full circle to the question you should ask yourself continually: If 20 percent of your clients generate 80 percent of your business, do you invest 80 percent of your time on that 20 percent? To generate the qualified referrals that will allow you to build a quality practice, you need to do exactly that. Right sizing your clientele will allow you to do it.

If you haven't already done so, the first thing to do in right-sizing your practice is to properly classify your clients. Through the process of classification, you will create a Triple-A ideal client profile which will allow you to identify the type of clients that you wish to work with.

Most advisors tell me that they've already classified their clients, but upon closer inspection, they've only done a partial job, because their only classification criterion was assets. I encourage you to engage in a more detailed client classification by using our Triple-A approach, and we'll take a deeper dive into just what that means. Throughout, be panoramic and all-encompassing in how you define your ideal client.

Triple-A: Defining your ideal client

To revisit definitions briefly, the first A in Triple-A speaks to **assets.** What asset level and range of needs must your clients have for them to be considered a good fit for your areas of expertise? Most advisors stop at this stage of client classification, but it is only the first step if you want to successfully right-size your practice.

The second A refers to **attitude**, which, over the lifetime of your working relationship, is actually more important than assets. What is their attitude toward you? Do they focus on what you cost or what you are worth? What is their attitude about empowerment? Do they treat you like a personal CFO, or do they insist on having investments with other advisors? Do they have an informed attitude about the way the markets work? Do they try to micromanage you? Are they disrespectful to your staff?

Keep in mind, assets change but attitudes rarely do. I have seen an advisor work with a client with great assets and a bad attitude, many times. In the long run, this client winds up hurting the advisor more than they help them.

An ideal client is someone who is enlightened. They buy into your process and they are therefore not "freaked-out" by volatility when the market goes up like an escalator and down like an elevator. Your attitudes are aligned and they know you'd never ask a client to do something you wouldn't do, yourself.

Alignment of attitude is powerful.

The third A stands for **advocacy**. Your top clients will frequently recommend your services. Ideal clients appreciate the merit of buying into a relationship with a professional consultant rather than buying products from a salesperson. They are extremely loyal and they feel they are doing a like-minded friend a disservice by not introducing them to you.

After completing this client classification process, you will be able to identify three types of clients we've already defined: Customers, clients and advocates. The value of your business has virtually nothing to do with how many clients you have and everything to do with how many advocates you have. In fact, as my story of the advisor with 900 customers shows, the ideal financial services practice consists of about 150 advocates, not a collection of 500 customers and clients.

Once you have created an ideal client profile, you need to commit to following it. When meeting with prospective clients, I suggest that you explain that you use an ideal client profile, and that you outline the three As. Include these topics on your meeting agenda, and explain why these features make you unique. Here is a script you can adapt to introduce the topic:

I've made the commitment to be a specialist rather than a generalist and, as a result, I am very selective about the clients I work with. Unlike some advisors who are trying to build a big business, and who attempt to be all things to all people, I prefer to be all things to some people. I know my capacity, and if I go beyond that level, it will dilute the service I provide. I can't allow that to happen. While some advisors are fixated on making a sale, I'm concerned that there be a fit between us, because I believe that is the foundation of a successful long-term working relationship. It is for that reason I have an ideal client profile, and that I stick to it.

How Big You Can Get, or How Small You Can Stay?

How many times have you heard the phrase, "It's not the quantity but the quality that matters"? This is definitely true when considering a professional advisor's book of business.

Despite this, a large number of advisors have a difficult time grasping the concept that bigger is not necessarily better. In fact, more often than not, advisors dream of building a large client base. One thing is for sure, in this day and age; a large book of business means considerably more work. Gone are the days where an advisor could be assured that a client is competitor-proofed with an annual or bi-annual call.

Client right-sizing is one of the first areas I tackle when working with someone in our one-to-one coaching program. It is often a difficult subject to broach, as many advisors going through our Pareto Systems program are looking for guidance to grow their businesses in order to increase their net incomes. Instinctively, they believe their action plan should begin with increasing the number of clients in their book, not paring down the number, and this is where many advisors miss the mark.

Are you looking to boost your income by increasing the size of your client base? If so, you should consider some important questions. Before answering, think hard about what each question implies:

- Could your business, as it is run now, handle a dramatic increase in new clients?

- Would a substantial increase in business create some level of chaos in your office? As you know, there is a lot involved in bringing on even one new client (or at least there should be!)

- Would an influx of new clients result in a decreased level of service for all your clients as a whole?

- Would you need to add an assistant to the team in order to keep track of all your clients and make sure that nothing falls through the cracks?

- Might the new business cause you to lose focus on the clients who matter most in your book, your top 20 percent? And if, as a result, you lost even a handful of your top clients, would that have a dramatic effect on your practice?

There is a specific process to growing one's business. It is often important for a professional to reduce their number of clients before adding new ones. The goal is to clear out the old, poorly-matched ones to make way for the new (and improved) clients. This gives the advisor the opportunity to let go of clients who aren't necessarily adding to his or her income but are certainly draining time, or have attitudinal qualities that don't align with the advisor's.

If you take anything from this section, please remember that to increase your income, you don't necessarily need more clients, just better and more engaged clients. Another thing to consider is that you could likely reduce your client base by letting go of clients who are not significantly contributing to your business, and remain at your current income level.

As I recently told an advisor client, your business has a long tail. Take the tail off, it's not essential or helpful – and don't let it grow back.

How long is the tail on your business?

To begin client right-sizing it is important that you first take a hard look at your client base after classification and make some critical decisions.

Who is your ideal client? Who is no longer suitable as a client? Who takes up too much of your time? As you can imagine, by re-evaluating who an ideal client may be, then letting go of the clients who don't (and most likely always won't) fit the bill, you become much more efficient. Let's face it; some clients are more of a hassle than they should be. They may eventually cause you to lose focus on the clients who deserve your full attention and your valuable time.

With a tighter correlation between the relationships you manage and the money you manage, you are able to gain control of your practice. By going through this process, you are now in a position where you are able to fully service your top clients.

When you spend more quality time with the clients who count, they begin to appreciate your services, regardless of what is happening with the market. As long as you are in constant contact with your top clients, they will feel as though you are looking out for their needs. If, at the same time, you are in the habit of re-stating your introduction process, those same top clients will brag about you to their friends and family. This will increase your rate of introductions and, soon enough, your number of ideal clients.

So, before haphazardly taking on new clients, remember that too much is as bad as not enough!

The Upside of Rightsizing: Bigger isn't Better

When I coach an advisor who has hit a plateau (often self-imposed), a quick step I will ask him or her to take is to analyze a typical week in their life. In other words, how many hours do they work, how many people do they meet in person and speak with on the phone, and what reactive and proactive activities do they see through consistently?

As always, our activities determine our productivity. Furthermore, we are creatures of habit and those habits compound - and sometimes they can cause us to drift off track. That being said, is there a chance that you are spending time with clients who *demand* your attention at the expense of the clients who *deserve* your attention?

On the whole, your clients will break into three major strata:

1. **The replicable top** - You probably have 20 ideal clients and you'd like to have 50 of them.
2. **The movable middle** - Lots of untapped opportunity here in terms of empowerment and advocacy.
3. **The questionable bottom** - Clients who are generating low revenue and a high hassle-factor.

When you drill down, especially with a questionable client, often the issue is not a lack of assets but rather the existence of a flawed attitude. They question fees, are rude or disrespectful to staff, they micromanage, they are unrealistic about returns or the ways the markets work, have painfully high levels of self-importance, etc. When it comes to right-sizing, this is where you should start.

When I coach an advisor on the concept of right-sizing, the advisor often starts talking about the clients he or she wants to "fire". That's not what this is about. Ultimately, the client is not a good fit and you are doing them and yourself a disservice by keeping them. You want to take the high road and disassociate professionally and respectfully. Follow these four steps:

1. Identify the clients that are not a good fit using Triple-A.

2. Identify your options: Call center, sell, introduce to another advisor or disassociate from the client.

3. Develop and deploy a professional transfer process.

4. Be forthright in communicating the *why* and *how* to the soon-to-be-former client.

One of two things will happen at the moment of truth. Either the client will agree with you and cooperate fully, or they will take it personally and try to convince you that they should stay.

If you are clear and forthright about your rules of engagement, occasionally you can elevate a client to advocate status by going through this exercise. More often than not though, your instincts will have been correct and you will find yourself sounding like a broken record responding to every plea with, *"I just don't think there is a good fit going forward and I'd like to introduce you to some options that I feel are in your best interest."*

Sit down and tally up your Knock-Out Factors; traits and habits you don't want to work with long-term. Begin to examine both who you are working with and new possibilities in light of these factors. Things like:

You dread answering the call when this number pops up on your phone.

You flinch when you see their name on your upcoming calendar.

They're a jerk.

They are disrespectful.

They are a micro-manager.

They constantly focus on what you cost, not what you're worth.

They panic at every market shift.

And so on. Be honest with yourself.

For many advisors the ideal business is about 150 clients. For some it is more, for some less, but as an average, 150 is a good number. If you want to increase the amount of money you are managing, you may need to take another hard look at your client base and lower the number of relationships you are managing. In addition to better, more profitable and enjoyable relationships, rightsizing restores liberation and order to your personal life.

Again, the goal is not to see how big you can get, but rather how small you can stay.

Get it Out of Your Head

The key is to take all of this from a concept in your head and galvanize your vision and deliverables on paper for you, your team, and your clients to see. None of what you do is an asset or an intellectual property unless it's documented. If it's in your head, it's just a concept.

Create a series of integrated documents that people can hold in their hands that demonstrate that you are professional consultant who strives to be all things to some people, rather than a salesperson who tries to be all things to all people.

When you show a client your ideal client profile, complete with all the attitudinal qualities you are looking for, you take the abstract nature of who is a good fit and turn it into something that is much easier to understand and communicate.

When you show them, rather just explain to them, how you plan to consistently communicate with and service a client based on the distinctions between AAA, AA, A or B, C, or D clients, you do two things. Not only do you make yourself more compelling and referable to more AAA clients, you also get on the path of least resistance in terms of attracting new business based on money in motion and evolving needs, as opposed to chasing new sales opportunities.

The knowledge-for-profit industries have been primarily a sales-centered culture for many years and your clients have been on the receiving end of that. Craft a process that breaks that old dynamic.

Right-Sizing is Seldom the Wrong Thing to Do

We're all familiar with the concept of supply and demand. The more scarce the supply, the more demand increases, as does the perceived or actual value of what you supply.

What do you supply? It's not just your investment knowledge. That's becoming more commoditized every day. What you are supplying is your time. So the question is, do you project scarcity and have a process to ensure that the perceived value for your time continues to grow? Asked another way, do your clients feel accomplished when you accept them as a client? Are they buying investments from you, or are they buying into a meaningful relationship with you? You can turn back a page or two and revisit *What is Your Capacity* if you're not on the same wavelength, here.

Let's drill down a little deeper. Based on where you are today, are you on- or off-track in terms of where you thought you'd be at this stage of your life? Are you, today, where you predicted you'd be five years ago? Are you getting closer to your goals or do you feel that you are drifting away from them?

I'm asking you these questions because they are the same questions I ask an elite advisor when they approach me to inquire about our coaching program. It's still incredible to me that the people who like coaching the most typically need it the least. They are already successful, but they feel they still have more to accomplish. Their aspiration is almost insatiable but sometimes it can take them down the wrong path.

Michael Gerber said it best in The E-Myth: "Your business is supposed to be serving your life, not the other way around." As practice management consultants to some of the best professional advisors in the business, we've helped advisors break old patterns and focus on the specific factors that contribute to building a business that is profitable and restores liberation and order.

For advisors that have hit a plateau, I examine a variety of issues that could be undermining their progress. More often than not, I find these advisors either have too many clients or they haven't effectively deployed systems and procedures that ensure they are allocating their time and efforts to the most deserving clients. Among other issues, a by-product of this is that clients are unclear about who is a good fit for the advisor, and as a result there is a disconnect in their understanding of the type of person they should be referring their advisor to.

Another benefit of classifying clients is that you can then use a service matrix to ensure that you consistently meet and exceed the expectations you've set for the various tiers of clients. It also gives both you and your clients clarity of understanding as to who is a good fit for you, and creates an aspirational environment that ensures that clients want to work with you and value your service and skill-set.

Your Rules of Engagement

An important dimension to the right sizing process – and this is where Knock-Out Factors are critical - is to get clarity on your rules of engagement and then to stick with them going forward. Here is a simple checklist to ensure you're on the right track:

Define your ideal client based on assets, attitude and advocacy and determine who fits and who doesn't. Define your Knock-Out Factors - all the client issues that are not acceptable going forward.

Define how you allocate time. Clearly define times when you return calls. Insure you are not randomly taking calls. Clearly define time frames for meetings. How much time off you will take, etc.

Be forthright with clients. When onboarding new clients or in a review meeting with existing clients, refer to this item on your meeting agenda and explain why you take this approach and the impact it has on service, focus and consistency.

The above is not to take away from your commitment to service, but I want your clients to value your availability. The best way to take care of your clients is to take impeccable care of yourself. By rounding out your ideal client profile with specific Rules of Engagement that include Knock-Out Factors, you keep reminding yourself how valuable your time is and how important it is not to establish relationships with clients that don't align well with you.

There are countless cases where an advisor has gone through this process and created more capacity to better serve existing advocate relationships, attracted new high-quality clients, projected scarcity and netted all the other practical benefits that come with this. For me, though, the biggest reward occurs when an advisor is rejuvenated and reaches a point where he or she starts running the business instead of the other way around.

Recently, a good advisor-client of ours told me about a $3.5 million problem client who was right-sized. The hassle factor kept ratcheting upwards and the advisor had finally had enough. She right-sized professionally and felt liberated along the way. The symbolic benefit this had on her staff was substantial, too.

No hero story would be complete without telling you that within 90 days, this advisor replaced the assets with two new ideal clients who were introduced to her by existing advocates.

Revisiting the Law of Environment

I was first exposed to *The Law of Environment* in the 80's movie *Trading Places*. Once it was on my radar I started noticing how powerful an influence the people we associate with are on our outlook, mindset and behavior.

Warren Buffet said it well. "There are three qualities to look for in people: Integrity, intelligence and energy, and if they don't have the first, the other two will kill you."

Just so there is no mistake: *Everything* you do is client-centered, whether meeting with a client's friend, recruiting a protégé or conveying the full array of your services. Everything is client-centered, including right-sizing. If you have too many clients, or clients you cannot stand working with, no one wins, and that has to be the core principle that governs right-sizing.

Never wrestle with a pig. You both get dirty, but the pig likes it - George Bernard Shaw

The Art of Manufacturing Capacity: How to be More Efficient with Your B Clients

There are times and situations in some businesses that do not allow for right-sizing. So here's a great alternative – focus on being worthy of your fees and define client service expectations.

In addition to strengthening your client relationships and running a more efficient and productive business, the process of developing a "Fee-Worthy" mindset and approach can provide you with another meaningful benefit. You also become more efficient with your time. With money we think of Return on Investment; with time we should be thinking about ROE - Return on Energy.

The Smartest Don't Work the Hardest

I've seen it time and time again. Being more productive doesn't mean that you have to work harder or put in longer hours. You just have to be strict and economical with your time.

You do it every day, without thinking about it. When you buy a power screwdriver to replace your rusty old manual one, you are buying time. You are focused on accomplishing the same job but in less time and with less energy expended.

As I identified earlier, one way to manufacture capacity, free up time and reduce hassle factors is to right-size your client base. Focusing on how small you can stay has worked wonders for several advisors who hit a plateau, but that isn't to say it is necessary for every advisor. Some advisors transfer B and C clients to a Call Center. Others hire a protégé to manage B clients to free themselves up to provide enhanced service to A clients.

Another approach is to come back to the Pareto Principal. If 80 percent of your business is stemming from 20 percent of your clients then you must invest 80 percent of your time with those clients on a one-to-one basis. And if 20 percent of your business is coming from 80 percent of your clients perhaps a one-to-many approach for your B clients using a managed money platform is the answer.

You've probably considered a managed money platform for a block of your B clients but never executed on the concept. I can tell you this - and this stems from countless observations - done properly, following a predictable and sustainable process that is positioned professionally and as a benefit to your clients, this can manufacture time and capacity to ensure that the business serves your life.

The key in that statement is that you *position the concept as a benefit* to your B clients. I say that because many advisors feel that the optics (from the clients' perspective) of transitioning all or even just a block of B clients to a managed money program will be negative. Surely clients will feel they are being trivialized and will eventually defect to another advisor? I'm here to tell you that it all comes down to how you position it. Not to oversimplify it, but you can follow this simple checklist as a starting point:

- **Research** - It should go without saying, but scrutinize the platforms available to you and be in no hurry to select one that is the best fit.

- **Apply a two-meeting approach** - The first meeting is for introducing the concept and the second is for the actual transition itself.

- **The importance of process** - Explain the difference between a financial plan and on-going financial planning.

This is the recipe for the secret sauce, for lack of a better analogy. With your B clients, you want to explain how this is a proactive and ongoing process that helps you both take a long view to financial planning while at the same time still being nimble enough to react to fluctuations and external events along the way.

Many clients think of financial planning as a one-off event where the advisor diagnoses the client's issues, identifies their goals and objectives and then creates a 120-page plan that the client probably won't read or understand but might feel better simply holding.

True financial planning is a fluid and dynamic process that can be affected greatly by Critical Life Events; any one of which can instantly render that 120-page plan obsolete. When you are transitioning your relationship to a managed money approach, you can re-frame the client's understanding of your role in their life. It is one thing to explain the difference between transactional commissions and transparent asset management fees, but a Fee-Worthy Advisor goes deeper than that.

The Fee-Worthy Advisor uses words like "process", "consistency" and "predictability" - not in terms of returns on a statement but in terms of advisor-client engagement. They use metaphors like the weather, a GPS and the seasons to help the client conceptualize how the advisor navigates through storms and seasonal swings. The markets are like the weather - you can anticipate some storms and others you cannot. The markets are like the seasons. You can count on the seasons of life but the severity of each season can fluctuate from year to year.

This can help your clients truly understand your role and your value and see past turbulent periods.

Many advisors say that having a Fee-Worthy mindset puts you on the same side of the table as your client. I say that it puts you both on the same wavelength, and that understanding competitor-proofs your clients, minimizes their anxieties about external factors and events and improves your refer-ability. It also has proven to dramatically reduce the daily frequency of inbound client calls because of their renewed confidence in you and your process, and that takes the transitional process from time well spent to the best investment you'll ever make.

Never Negotiate Your Value: Focus on Worth, Not Fees

One of the most important attitudinal qualities of an ideal client is that they appreciate your value and don't question your fees. You know there are some people who resent your fees. That is sometimes due to the fact that you weren't forthright about your fees and they became aware of them later. You have to own that so that you never have a client calling you asking "My accountant just informed me that I paid you $70,000 in fees last year. Is that accurate?"

What about new clients and fees? Especially during turbulent and uncertain market conditions, there is a tendency for financial professionals to deviate on their set pricing and fees due to fear of losing out on new clients.

How do you respond when a prospective client says something like this to you? "I've met with two of your competitors and they have both offered to lower their fees in order to get my business."

Ultimately, it's your business and you live by the rules you set. However, allow me to outline my case for maintaining consistency.

First of all, and especially during anxious economic times, it is far easier for a professional to stand out from the pack. Prospective clients spend more time contrasting potential new service providers and you can use this reality as an opportunity to differentiate yourself from others.

Chances are, your competitors will amplify their salesmanship and in the process project a high degree of neediness and desperation to prospective clients. A more professional consultative approach where you focus on mutual fit, rather than just making a sale, is far more attractive, especially to high-caliber potential clients.

When a prospective client realizes that you are focused on the lifetime value of a relationship rather than on an immediate commission, you project scarcity and disarm them so that they are far more predisposed toward you. It positions you as a superior alternative.

At the critical moment of truth when someone asks you to lower your fees, you have to convey your rules of engagement with an understated calm:

"You know, I hear where you're coming from. Especially in these market conditions we all want to be shrewd in terms of how we invest our money. However, you need to know that I never negotiate my value. You see, someone who is prepared to lower their fees is simply trying to make a sale. They are solely focused on commissions. That isn't my approach. I focus on long term relationships based on trust and I think if price is what's really important to you, you run the risk of overlooking what is utterly important in this type of relationship over the long haul. So I'm probably not the provider for you because I never negotiate my value."

Another important question to consider is this: Do you want to do business with someone who is completely focused on getting something cheap? The relationship is going to last long after you've spent the money you'll earn on the initial fees, and how you start a relationship ultimately impacts how it will unfold over the long haul.

This approach doesn't work every time, but, then again, it shouldn't. Not everyone is a good fit for you and you have to be selective in terms of the type of client you strive to attract. When someone knows where you stand, you radiate professionalism and in the process your story becomes easy for a client to tell a friend or family member. People crave consistency and professionalism and those factors serve as the foundation of refer-ability.

To give a specific example, here's a simple story to illustrate the point of understanding one's value. A wealthy homeowner contacted a plumber complaining about some pipes that were rattling in his majestic yet aging mansion. The plumber walked in, quickly surveyed an array of pipes, calmly took out a hammer and tapped in one specific area of the pipe network. Sure enough, the rattling stopped. The plumber pulled out his invoice book and wrote out a receipt for $500. When the homeowner objected and demanded an explanation for what appeared to be an excessive fee for a simplistic task, the plumber methodically wrote these words: *$20 for hitting pipes, $480 for knowing where to hit.*

How you start a relationship will have a profound impact on how well it plays out. If a prospective client tells you they're not comfortable empowering you fully, what are your rules of engagement? As one advisor puts it; when a prospective client says that they are uncomfortable empowering this advisor fully and putting "all their eggs in one basket", the advisor's rules of engagement are clear: "If you think of me as a basket, it's not a good fit."

The Service Matrix Makes You Fee-Worthy

I stress worth as the measure you need to be judged by, rather than cost. Let's delve into how a Service Matrix can help smooth your route through transitions or troubled times and encourage clients to see you as worthy of your compensation while, at the same time, ensuring that you are investing your time on the clients who generate 80 percent of your income.

First off, if you are like most professional advisors, you have a team of associates and assistants helping you run your business profitably and efficiently. You undoubtedly have strategic planning sessions to kick your own tires and identify untapped opportunities, areas for refinement, miscues and the like. Whether these sessions are held weekly, monthly or quarterly in your office, or even yearly at an off-site retreat, one of the key points of discussion should be "Do we deserve what we want?" Again, the word "deserve" stems from the Latin words "to serve".

In other words, is the level of service we provide in proportion to what we expect to earn from our client relationships? Having a service matrix helps ensure you are deserving.

In your next team meeting set aside some time to go through the following process to build your Service Matrix; a listing of all the services you provide that identifies which clients receive which services based on their classification.

Clearly a Triple-A client will receive every form of service you provide. They deserve it. A Double A client will receive every form of service you provide as well because they could be on the verge of Triple-A status, but a Single-A, B, C or D client will not receive the same level of service.

You can't be all things to all people. A Service Matrix ensures you are all things to some people.

Here are the steps to creating a Service Matrix:

- List all your proactive and reactive services - everything from call rotations, to holiday or birthday cards to review meetings and client events. Get them out of your heads and list them. You'll be shocked and impressed at the length of the list.

- Identify who on your team provides each service deliverable - let there be no doubt about who is accountable. This is an essential step to consistency and predictability.

- Ensure the services are documented in your Playbook. Empower your staff to document each process into a best-practice and turn it into an intellectual property.

- Apply your client classification - AAA clients receive everything, AA clients receive everything, A, B and C clients receive less.

- Be clear about your rules of engagement - identify client qualities you hope to attract and traits that you have no interest in.

- Establish recurring services. Use a CRM to create automated processes for recurring activities to create efficiency and ensure nothing falls through the cracks.

Once you have completed this process, be consistent and clear in your execution and communication. You aren't being elitist or disrespectful; you are ensuring that your clients receive the level of service they deserve. Along the way you will earn the right to expect your best clients' loyalty, empowerment and advocacy.

Getting back to compensation for a moment, in review meetings with existing clients and in fit meetings with prospective clients it is essential that you communicate your compensation in a proactive manner. It's on their minds so take the mystery away by discussing it in a casual yet prepared manner. In the process, you can create an aspirational environment when you outline that you have a service matrix and project scarcity because of your approach to providing the highest levels of service to the most deserving clients.

It's amazing how much opportunity can be uncovered by explaining your code-of-conduct and commitment to best practices.

So what do you do when a Single-A client with great assets, a poor attitude and no advocacy discovers that they aren't invited to a client event or don't get taken out for lunch on their birthday? You apologize for not being forthright about your commitment to best practices and explain that you have a service matrix that ensures that your very best clients receive an enhanced level of service. Say this:

"I apologize for not being clear about this until now, but I made a decision that I wouldn't try to be all things to all people but rather all things to some people. My most deserving clients are those who align with my ideal client profile based on Assets that fit my expertise, an Attitude that is complementary with mine and a mindset of Advocacy meaning they feel compelled to introduce friends and family members to me as our relationship unfolds. And while you've been a great client in terms of Assets, we've had some issues regarding chemistry and you've never been inclined on the Advocacy side. I should have been clearer about how I pay tribute and say thanks to my Triple-A clients."

Don't be surprised if your Single-A clients says, "That's all it takes to be a Triple-A client? It never occurred to me to introduce people to you because I didn't even know you were accepting new clients. I want to take our relationship to the next level."

If it turns out that the relationship isn't destined to move to that next level, that revelation can be a positive, too. Many advisors tell me that everything changed for them the moment they told a prospective client there wasn't a fit or disassociated from a high maintenance client. At the moment of truth, when you are at the go/no-go stage, when your heart, instincts and intellect are telling you "This relationship is not going to play out well" and you start pulling away and inform that person that "I don't think I'm the advisor for you", you activate the first step in the process of restoring liberation and order to your life.

Make Compliance Your Friend: Be Compliant for What it Gets You, Not Because You Have To

You might be wondering how the topic of compliance relates to productivity. Many people shudder at the thought of compliance and consider it to be a major hurdle when it comes to client acquisition and business development in general. In fact, I have a client that refers to the compliance department at his firm as the "Sales Prevention Squad".

Hear me out, because I am convinced in light of experience that changing your mindset about compliance can be an integral component to success in business.

Often in conversations with professional advisors about the realities of compliance, I like to focus on the benefits the advisor will realize as opposed to their obligations. I say that because not only does a compliant professional advisor project more professionalism through their consistent conduct - leading to increased loyalty, empowerment and advocacy - they also get to sleep soundly at night.

I'm mentioning this because I recently had yet another conversation with a professional advisor who had a client who made untrue claims that were startling and a little scary. This advisor was a user of relationship management technology and fortunately he followed our process to address the claims during the audit and investigation.

During the audit, the advisor gave the investigator access to his Client Relationship Management solution to review the relationship journal, history and communications track and in short order he was cleared of all accusations. You see, in addition to telling our clients to invest every conversation into the bigger relationship - meaning to capture and chronicle everything that is exchanged on a phone call or meeting - we also explain why this crucial information must be archived in a format that is time-stamped and can't be altered or erased. If you can alter your client communication history, you are not compliant, and you are at risk in this hyper-litigious era.

To us, though, this is where being compliant just gets started. Yes, you want to archive all emails, documents and various forms of communications in a sequential and search-able format that is easy to access. But you can support that with a panoramic K.Y.C. (Know Your Client) process. I suggest using F.O.R.M., which we've touched on multiple times, as the driving force. As a client relationship unfolds and you uncover and then capture and chronicle F.O.R.M. information, you create a holistic window into the client's core motivations, philosophy, relationship mindset and much more.

This goes so far beyond just understanding their risk tolerance, financial goals and overall financial awareness, because you get to know the entire person. The portrait you create of the total client reinforces how your wealth management strategy is tailored specifically to that client. It speaks volumes about your overall approach. Furthermore, the F.O.R.M. profiling process enables you to develop chemistry and develop a deeper bond that can help insulate you from factors out of your control.

Remember, the relationship lasts long after you spend the money you made on the initial fees. So take action and protect yourself. You already know that some people will use you as a lightning rod to channel their frustrations in life. Some people have an aversion to responsibility and find a warped sense of satisfaction in blaming others. Ultimately, some people have a selective memory for specific events that don't unfold as they hoped.

Be compliant in the way you conduct yourself, and be consistent in the type of client you attract and you will have the ultimate S.W.A.N. business - one that serves your life and lets you Sleep Well At Night.

The Best Way to Improve What You Do is to Listen to the People You Do it For

Listening has come up again and again in this book. Queue the broken record and let's drill down as to why this is vitally important, and how you can draw out the information that will be of the most value to you in building relationships and encouraging advocacy.

Listening doesn't just make a client confident and happy; it gives you real information that makes you better in turn. It's possible for your judgment to be clouded by inertia confidence, by neglect or by getting into a feedback vacuum. Your clients are the best board of directors/advisory panel you can have. They will keep you on track.

All elite professionals understand the importance of ongoing personal and business development. Top performers know that they have to continually sharpen their skills. To earn more we have to learn more, but it can be a challenge to make the time and to measure the ROI. That said, as the metaphor reminds us, you can never be so busy cutting wood that you can't make time to sharpen your saw.

You might think I'm going to recommend that you attend seminars and boot camps, hire a coach, read books and participate in virtual learning programs to improve your skills and deliverables. All of those options are fine, but before you ever listen to an outsider giving you advice, listen to your clients. They are far better equipped to tell you what you need to do to improve. As Mark Twain said, "The customer is the only critic whose opinion really counts."

There is yet another win-win outcome when you listen to your clients. Not only do you get a clear sense of how they perceive you (and describe you to others) but you also can use this information to drive business. The ideas that spark from your focused listening can create an invaluable foundation for on-going client acquisition. We've seen several advisors achieve meaningful breakthroughs using some of these simple strategies.

You can start with a low-key, informal survey using probing questions during your next round of client call rotations. As you know, I recommend that you consistently reach out to your best clients via the telephone as part of your ongoing service process. As you also know, I suggest that you approach each call with the goal of being interested rather than trying to be interesting. You aren't calling to sell something or be the bearer of profound news or insight. You are just touching base and asking good questions. This is about competitor-proofing and long-term relationship management.

You want the initial questions to be about the client and their F.O.R.M. information, but there is a natural segue in every call where you can shift the focus to *you* while still asking their opinion. For example:

1. To get a sense for their satisfaction and loyalty: *What's the one thing that you value most about our relationship?* Or - *If there was any one thing we could add to improve the client experience, what would it be?*

2. To see if they understand everything you do and provide: *Have we done an effective job explaining our full array of services?*

3. To get the client thinking about people they could introduce: *When you talk about me with a friend, what do you say? How do you describe me?*

It's a good idea to start a question with this simple softening statement: *If you don't mind me asking...*

You can then clarify the question with a little more detail by saying: *The reason I'm asking is...*

The key here is that you aren't marketing to yourself. It's easy to get into a bit of a vacuum with your business development efforts and lose objectivity. These questions engage clients so that you can get a sense of where you stand.

From a loyalty perspective, your clients are exposed to countless competing messages. You want to show them that you don't take them for granted. From a money-in-motion perspective, your clients' needs are constantly evolving. As a new need presents itself, you want the client to instantly think of you as the person to fill that need. From an advocacy perspective, you don't know when a referral opportunity will come about, but when it does you want to be top of mind with your clients so that they will be compelled to endorse you.

When you are talking to your clients, you can amplify the impact by telling them the motivation behind your questions by saying this:

"I always want to try to raise the bar in terms of the service I provide and the best way to improve my service is to talk to the people who are receiving it. That is where the best new ideas will come from."

Or: *"We've recently hired a consultant to assist us with enhancing the client experience and we want to hear what clients would most like to see from us going forward."*

The point is to do the above *continually* to prove you're *acting* on the input and not just dabbling or going through the motions.

Now, those are just a few one-to-one ideas to get you started, but if you want to take this concept to a one-to-many level, you might consider hosting a Client Advisory Council. This is a concept we've been helping top advisors execute for several years and it has been invaluable from a loyalty, empowerment and endorsement perspective.

The idea is simple. You invite a small group of your favorite clients together for breakfast on a Saturday morning or dinner on a weeknight. You have an agenda of questions and you probe away. It is incredible what these events can reveal in terms of how you are perceived and described to others and for the untapped opportunities that can be uncovered.

From a target marketing and client acquisition perspective, you can conduct a focused Client Advisory Council. If you want to target more business owners, conduct a CAC with the business owner clients you currently have and say this:

"I value my relationships with business owners more than you can know. When I became a professional advisor I attracted a variety of new clients from different walks of life, but going forward I really want to be a specialist rather than a generalist. Some advisors try to be all things to all people. I would rather be all things to some people, and those people are business owners. They have needs that perfectly fit my areas of expertise now and as their lives unfold. And, frankly they are just simply good, hardworking, interesting people. That said, I'd like to ask you questions outlined in this agenda that can start a conversation that can help me become attractive and indispensable to more business owners just like yourself."

Make your clients the voice you listen to. Just as importantly, demonstrate that you're acting on their feedback. Close the feedback loop by continually pointing to any surveys or input you sought from your clients, and show them the actions you're taking. This takes it from a claim that you'll be improving the client experience, to your clients actually appreciating the elevation of service.

When you ask for money, you get advice. When you ask for advice, you get money – Start-up truism

---

Hail, No!

The essence of this book is to work more closely with the people who are already convinced, rather than trying to grow your business by convincing new people. This is all an extension of how you are perceived and described – to not only improve client loyalty but to also improve refer-ability.

If nothing else, I want to make sure you differentiate between marketing and branding. I don't know how many times I've seen someone stall and then grasp at a marketing tactic that was nothing more than a Hail Mary.

Doug Flutie threw, arguably, the most famous game-winning touchdown pass in US college football history in 1984. "The Pass", as it became known, helped underdog Boston College defeat the heavily favored University of Miami Hurricanes led by Bernie Kosar.

While everyone loves an underdog, and everyone loves the drama of a last-minute scoring drive to win a big game, obviously the Hail Mary is not a predictable proposition. In the decades since The Pass, how many times have you seen the Hail Mary work? It's incredibly rare.

I say that because, in business, I see professional advisors lose faith in simple, proven practice management and business development disciplines and instead engage in flawed marketing tactics that promise instant results but often fail to produce anything more than disappointment. In other words, they throw a Hail Mary.

I see professional advisors cold-call perfect strangers rather than do a call rotation for existing clients. I see advisors do prospecting seminars rather than a client advisory council or client appreciation event, and I see advisors run advertising campaigns rather than network with existing strategic allies and other professional influencers.

"Spray and pray" marketing strategies are flawed on so many levels. Why, then, do so many advisors still attempt them? The reason for this is simple; nurturing existing relationships and other tried and true strategies can be boring and rarely results in instant gratification. Too many advisors want to find the next "new idea", something with some "sizzle", and, as a result, are continually searching for and dabbling with concepts that ultimately have minimal impact.

It's not unlike investing. How many times have you seen someone try to hit a home-run with a high-risk investment opportunity rather than stick with a methodical long-term approach?

It's not just money that compounds. As I've said before, discipline compounds, too. You have to be patient and let your efforts gather momentum. Too many advisors get themselves into the proverbial "Red Zone" and, rather than stick to the plan and see it through, they self-sabotage by abandoning the fundamentals and trying something new. Neglect also compounds. If we neglect our existing relationships it's only a matter of time before they'll be lured away and we'll have to throw our own Hail Mary.

Don't deviate from your process. Identify the most fundamentally sound and proven trust-building activities, stick with them and tune out all the other noise. It's much more effective to strengthen and nurture existing relationships over the long haul, rather than perpetually trying to start new ones. The prospecting treadmill is draining and you are building a business that is chaotic and unfocused.

Relationships are proprietary and are a big part of the equity that you are building in your business.

Visit **www.TheAdvisorPlaybook.com** for access
to the Playbook Implementation Program

Section 5: Refer-ability

Being Attractive to Your Ideal Clients

*A referral from a client is a tremendous compliment and a huge
responsibility that can never be taken lightly - Anonymous*

Being good at what you do is expected by a client. For clients to feel it would be a disservice to a friend *not* to make an introduction requires you to be better than good.

Providing an exemplary level of service and communicating your value with clarity allows clients to buy into a relationship with you, not just products from you. It lets you exceed their expectations. Being refer-able actually does lead to referrals.

In this section, I'll expand on specific processes and strategies you can use to build and focus your refer-ability with your ideal clients.

The Contrast Principle and P.A.S.

We've looked at how the *Contrast Principal* can be a tremendous ally when meeting with prospective clients. Ideally, your fit process is designed to clearly highlight your points of difference in terms of philosophy, planning strategy and process.

In the spirit of "facts tell, stories sell", there is an additional component you can add to your repertoire that uses social proof to help a client move into a referring advocate role, quickly and without any salesmanship. Social proof uses examples of other people in similar situations to the one you are describing. It triggers the contrast principle and clients can relate to the story, and relate it to people they know.

This is an especially powerful tool where referrals are concerned. When someone asks you how things are going, speak to your purpose and fulfillment using the P.A.S. (Problem-Agitate-Solution) concept:

"I'm basically living the dream. Just the other day I was introduced to a friend of a client who was going through a (insert critical life event here)."

Then, explain the Problem: *"This friend was completely overwhelmed with so many unexpected moving parts."*

Then, Agitate the problem: *"The biggest shocker was the imminent tax implications that this event triggered. That had this friend literally shaking with apprehension and uncertainty."*

Then explain your Solution: *"I can't tell you how rewarding it was to simply break it all down, apply a process and start chipping away at the issue. You could see the apprehension melting away. I really love what I do."*

Again, you're not asking for a referral. You're reminding the client about your sense of purpose, telling a story and putting the concept back on the radar. Furthermore, you can embed the P.A.S. concept into your re-framing process for clients, whatever your deliverable:

"There are many services we provide to our clients, some of which aren't relevant to you yet, but as your life unfolds, your needs will evolve. My process will put all the pieces of that puzzle together. It reminds me of a client who had a parent develop some serious complications and had to be moved into a care home. It got the client thinking about his own frailties and mortality and opted into a long term care policy for himself and his wife. It sounds trite, but he said to me that he feels better just having it, and that it's much better to have it and not need it than to need it and not have it."

Nowhere in that conversation did the advisor try to sell an insurance policy. He simply opened the client's mind about his full array of services and the concept of the planning process being fluid and dynamic. A static plan becomes obsolete the moment any material change occurs in a client's life. Having a future-pacing process that is proactive creates receptivity for review and assessment of the track a client is on.

Speaking of review meetings for strategic and tactical adjustments; every document has to go somewhere. The PFO binder I keep referring to is the ideal hub. When you re-frame a relationship with a client to introduce your full array of services, provide the client with a new tab with the listing of services and instruct them to put it into their binder as a critical path to build into future reviews.

The services and solutions are the building blocks, but the PFO and the future pacing process is the mortar that holds it all together. It's not just about capturing money in motion or gaining wallet share, this process is positioned as a benefit to the client rather than a sales opportunity. In keeping with converting customers into fully empowering clients, you reduce friction and get to draft behind the growing trust of a progressing relationship, and this leads you to an inception point where clients become referral-generating advocates.

Consider this analogy: Throughout Texas and Alberta there are old abandoned oil wells. Because of new technology, firms were able to go back to those wells to extract oil that had been inaccessible for years. When you craft a better client experience and a more compelling branding strategy, you can maximize long term, plateaued client relationships and get more oil from the well.

As another example, consider two dentists, both of whom are equally competent. One dentist performs services that meet your expectations. The other dentist has created a soothing waiting room that puts you at ease, has a massage therapist who will provide a foot rub in advance of a dental procedure and sends you a Thanksgiving card each year to pay tribute to your loyalty. Which dentist is easier to refer?

Now a dentist's ideal client profile likely isn't as substantial as yours. In fact, it's probably limited to the client having teeth and an ability to pay for the services. The point being, the more sophisticated the client and the services delivered the more important it is to create a referable client experience. The person endorsing you needs to feel proud and compelled to endorse you, and know exactly how endorsing you will ultimately reflect on them.

The more memorable the experience, the more you put the odds in your favor. It's the *Law of Probability*.

Looking for Referrals? Be Referable!

One of the golden rules of conversation is that people tend to discuss the things that exceed their expectations, or that fall below them. People seldom discuss the things that *meet* their expectations, because those types of things do not make for a good anecdote.

As an advisor, you have a suite of services that you offer and that people expect when they hire you. These are things like review meetings, phone calls, estate planning, investments, legal advice and so on. You can do all of those things extremely well, but does that make you referable? Doing a job well is commendable, but if you limit yourself to these core deliverables, you have effectively shut yourself out of the areas where most referrals come from.

Savvy advisors realize that the core deliverables that are expected of them are just meeting expectations, and that in itself does not make for an interesting conversation. He or she is compensated well for those core deliverables and life goes on. In other words, the likelihood that clients are out there chatting up this kind of advisor is slim.

Contrast the preceding to an advisor that does all those core deliverables very well, but then goes above and beyond that for his best clients. This advisor keeps meticulous records on all his clients' F.O.R.M. details, and then plans service activities around what his clients like to do. Perhaps that is a wine tasting event, or maybe a nice client dinner several times a year, or maybe even renting a movie theater and filling it up with clients and their families. You get the idea. When people's expectations are exceeded in these ways, they will tell the story for days to come.

I worked with one advisor who called those service deliverables his "Tabasco" items. They add a bit of flavor and spice to make what could be bland memorable. Any time he initiates these "Tabasco" service activities, he usually sees referrals follow shortly afterward, and for good reason, too. When clients are telling stories about how well they are treated, the people listening are contrasting that story with their own situation. If they are not as well served, and if the story is compelling and attractive, they may get a nagging feeling that they are in the wrong place, and think, *"Why doesn't my advisor do that kind of thing?"*

These are the moments where the majority of referrals and introductions are born. To the listener, the grass looks greener indeed, and it is in these situations that an introduction comes to life and results in a phone call to the superior advisor.

Where it starts to get interesting is when the advisor discusses his or her Introduction Process on a regular basis with those coveted clients that are receiving this top-notch service; continually reminding the client by triggering moments of recognition and awareness.

With a dedicated Introduction Process, the clients begin to understand that these referral moments occur all the time. Moments when a chance encounter with a friend or family member reveals a situation in which that person is not as well served by their current advisor. They also begin to understand that they are in a unique position to help. Better yet, the client knows precisely how to handle the situation, the correct steps to take, and how to get their friend or family member in front of the superior advisor.

No one is out there talking about how great your last review meeting was. Take a good look at your service matrix, and if it is lacking those types of "Tabasco" service items, identify which clients are deserving of such attention, and then start laying on the service. They will talk you up any chance they get.

It's human nature, after all.

The Fifth C: The Key Piece of the Referral Puzzle

Advisors ask me what it takes to be referable. My response is simple: It all comes down to trust. Clients and strategic partners have to trust that endorsing you will reflect positively on them in turn, but what does that mean, and how can you predictably and methodically create trust? Let's revisit the foundation of refer-ability, summed up in the four Cs.:

Credentials – Your skills as a professional advisor in terms of your judgment and the solutions you provide give you the credibility needed to foster trust.

Consistency – People crave consistency and your professional deployment of best practices helps you meet and exceed the expectations you set for your clients.

Chemistry – The rapport you develop using F.O.R.M., as well as your sincere and holistic interest in your clients' lives, creates comfort and chemistry.

Congruency – Doing what you say you will and conducting yourself as a professional consultant rather than as a salesperson means that you can attract rather than having to chase new business.

Many elite advisors who deploy the Four C's are still underwhelmed with the quality and quantity of referrals they see. The reason is simple - while they have laid down a foundation for refer-ability, they still find themselves in the red-zone but not in the Promised Land. The last piece of the puzzle is to create awareness for the concept of referrals in their on-going **Communication** (the fifth C) with their clients and rain-makers.

Just because you are referable due to your professional conduct, that doesn't mean that it will occur to your clients that they should introduce a friend to you. You have to continually *communicate* your value to them so that they make the connection.

Many top advisors are reluctant to ask for a referral, in part because of a subconscious fear of rejection, but primarily because they don't want to put their clients on the spot or potentially undermine the trust they have built. So they don't go there. They don't bring it up and just hope for the best.

I'll remind you that you don't need to ask for referrals. As you know by now, it is far more professional to position the concept of a referral as service you are providing *to* your clients rather than as a favor you are asking *of* your clients.

You don't need an elevator speech or special tactics to sell your clients on the concept of referring someone to you. Explain that you will make yourself available as a sounding board, explain why you do it and outline a simple process that your client can follow to make an introduction.

The Power of Reminding Your Clients

Being referable and communicating the concept of a client introducing a friend to you is an ongoing activity.

When I talk to an individual advisor I ask them why they don't get referrals. More often than not the response is "I don't get them because I don't ask for them." To which I say, "Perfect, because contrary to what you've been told, you should never ask for referrals."

At a recent conference, I had conversations with several top-caliber professional advisors about how to attract a higher quality and quantity of referrals from their best clients. Once again it was confirmed that the elite in this business don't use esoteric referral systems or pushy sales tactics. They remind their clients that they are available to meet with a friend, family member or business associate. What's more, these advisors have proved that they don't need to ask for referrals and look needy or desperate in the process. Instead, they subtly and repeatedly create awareness for their clients that they accept referrals and they position the concept as a service they are providing to them.

Ultimately you have to be referable in the first place by having good credentials, strong chemistry with clients, and consistent service driven by the habitual deployment of best practices, but the last number in the combination that has to be dialed-in to unlock your referral potential is communication. You have to talk about your process.

While every advisor has been told repeatedly at seminars and through coaching programs that they "should always be asking for referrals", many don't go there for the reasons I discussed, above. The distinction between salesmanship and stewardship is that a salesperson wants to impact their next paycheck and, as a result, they project a climate of expectation or obligation that the client needs to refer people. Consultants know that the lifelong value of a relationship is more valuable than occasional commissions, and they are more reserved. You can have better persuasive impact if you don't appear needy.

You want to create *awareness* of the concept of referrals. This is the first step in the process. You want to make sure that when that moment of truth occurs - when a friend asks your client, *"are you happy with your advisor?"* - that you are top-of-mind and easy for the client to endorse. Your process – your Nike Swoosh - comes immediately to their mind when a triggering interaction occurs.

Here are Four Pieces of the Awareness Puzzle:

1: Give them a reason to talk about referrals.

Nothing is more powerful than a client inquiring about the concept of referrals, or asking you if they can introduce someone to you. You can create that situation with gentle, subtle reminders.

For example, we've told many advisors to professionally frame and display this quote in their offices to serve as a trigger to get clients thinking about waving your flag: *"A referral from a client is a tremendous compliment and huge responsibility that can never be taken lightly."* You will be amazed at how many clients will say they didn't know you were accepting new clients. Best of all, you weren't the person who started the conversation. Their comment gives you permission to segue into your sounding-board value proposition.

2: Make it easy for clients to discuss referrals.

When you put someone on the spot and ask them for a referral, I believe it hurts you more than it helps you over the long haul. Conversely, when you create a relaxed atmosphere, you disarm the client and eliminate any tension or anxiety. Whenever you are discussing the concept of referrals, mention this: *"Keep in mind, if you ever happen to introduce someone to me, they do not need to become a client of mine to take advantage of my sounding board process."* You want your clients to feel relaxed and comfortable with the concept of making a call to you to introduce someone. You want your phone to ring. Your Fit process will take care of the rest.

3: Remind them forever.

In every form of communication you have with a client, remind them that you accept referrals without asking for them. Just keep putting it out there. In phone calls, review meetings, at events and in emails, remind them. Many advisors I work with add this tag at the bottom of their emails: *"Keep in mind that if you have a friend or family member who is anxious about their personal financial plan, they can take advantage of my Sounding Board Process – a one-hour consultation where I offer them feedback about the track they are on. It's a free value-added service that people find to be of real benefit."* You may only want to include that in emails to your best clients. This activity – based on the *Law of Cause and Effect* – leads to greater productivity. Keep reminding them and the stars will align for you.

4: Validate them by deploying an impeccable process driven by best practices.

Whenever a client or partner introduces you to someone, you know that, at some point down the road, those two people will talk and the experience you provided will come up in the conversation. Ensure that the person that was introduced says *"thank you!"* to the rainmaker. Your commitment to service prompts him or her to validate their delight to the person who referred them, and that validation opens the referral floodgates in the future.

Bottom line, don't ask for referrals. Communicate your value and position it properly. Reinforce it with a structure that speaks to the client's *why* with your purpose, to *who* they should be referring with a clear understanding of your ideal client Triple-A fit and the *how* of your introductory process.

Think of the last five things you recommended to a friend: A bottle of wine, a hairdresser, a vacation destination, a movie and a book. Did anyone ask you to make those referrals? You felt compelled to because you knew that the endorsement would benefit your friend and ultimately reflect well on you.

S.O.N.A.R. and Refer-ability

To give you an example of a referral process template in a more general sense, let's look at a fictional financial advisor using the S.O.N.A.R. process – a concept adapted from the book *How to Get Your Competition Fired* by Randy Schwantz. The process follows five steps as you speak with an existing client and keys off the *Contrast Principle,* with a focus on positioning that encourages the client to suggest they refer you to a friend, rather than you asking for a referral.

- **Situation:** Share a situation concerning an introduction that you recently received from another client, and tell them the story associated with that introduction.
- **Opportunity:** Tell the prospect what the opportunity was that you uncovered through that introduction.
- **Need:** Share the need you addressed for that client.
- **Action**: Speak to the specific action that you took for that family.
- **Result:** Conclude with the result of your action.

As you engage in this process remember that facts tell, stories sell. Here's a possible route for the conversation:

Client: *How is business? What have you been up to?*

Advisor: *Its funny you ask. We are on cloud nine right now! We just recently visited with a family that came to our group through an introduction from one of our most valued clients (that in and of itself makes us feel great) however, what we uncovered was truly mind boggling.*

Client: (Intrigued question)

Advisor: *This family was in an interesting situation that had them concentrated in a very large individual stock position. With a strong interest in philanthropic giving, they were in a unique position. We uncovered an opportunity to position part of this equity into a charitable trust. We introduced them to an estate planning partner who was able to create a trust with their specific intentions at heart, and the result was that millions of dollars that would have gone to taxes is now going to the John J. Smith foundation.*

Client: *Interesting, I wasn't aware you were still taking on new clients. It's not an uncommon issue that friends of mine find themselves trying to allocate their resources in the most tax efficient and meaningful manner. I wonder if you might be willing to share this strategy with them?*

The Law of Reciprocity: How Being Interested Makes You More Interesting

Whether you're speaking to a client or a strategic partner, you can improve your refer-ability by getting them to think about their *own* refer-ability. When you're having a conversation, ask them this question:

"The next time I'm talking to someone and the opportunity to wave your flag comes up, how would you like me to describe you?"

There is a good chance that your client or partner will say:

"I appreciate that. No one has ever asked me that before, but come to think about it the best thing to say would be this..."

You can then drill-down a bit and validate your question by saying:

"That's perfect. I'm asking you this because I have a pretty vast network and I'm always looking to make introductions where I see an opportunity and potential fit."

Inevitably your client or partner will ask:

"What is the best way for me to describe you when I get the opportunity in the future?"

This gives you permission to restate your value proposition and reinforce your personal branding strategy. You might say:

"Thanks for asking. As you know, I manage the wealth of a select few successful business owners across the country using a process that we've developed and refined through many cycles and market conditions."

If they inquire further, you can remind them that you make yourself available as a sounding board should they ever feel compelled to introduce a friend, family member or client to you in the future.

In keeping with not looking needy, frame the reminder with this phrase: *This is part of our process. It's a value-added service our clients find to be of benefit.*

Ultimately, this approach needs to be driven by a professional philosophy and mindset, not as a gimmick or tactic to drive sales. Sure, capitalism is rooted in self-interest, networking and endorsements, but you are trying to create a culture of value and awareness for referrals. That can be supported by proper positioning.

There is an old saying that giving starts the receiving process. The world is round and positive actions come back full circle to us in time. The beauty of this approach is that it doesn't make you look needy and congruently supports the premise of positioning a referral as a service you provide. It conveys your mindset: You like to identify opportunities where there might be an alignment of interests. In the process you attract referrals rather than chase them.

It's good karma to be looking out for your clients and partners while demonstrating that you are interested in them and are bringing value to them. The concept of advocacy appeals to our core drivers as business professionals. Think about it. When you ask someone the question, *"How's business?"* often, after they respond, they will ask you how business is for *you*.

Let me add one more scenario to reinforce this concept. Think of your favorite wholesaler. Sure, he or she knows their stuff and works for a good firm that provides good returns, but that isn't why he or she is your favorite wholesaler. They are your favorite because they are interested in your business and are often trying to add value beyond just good rates of returns.

The most consistent professionals in this business, who thrive in all conditions, don't live solely by the performance sword. They stand out and differentiate by being interested in their clients. This not only makes you memorable and referable - it makes you indispensable, too.

Increase Advocacy and Demonstrate Leadership during Uncertain Times

When it comes to market predictions, the media likes to stoke fear. They squeeze a topic for all it's worth and then zoom off to the next: Ebola, Y2K, elections, China meltdowns, terrorism, red food dye. Why? Fear and uncertainty achieve better ratings than good news and stability.

It's at such times that you are at your highest level of refer-ability. Money is topical, as is its management.

Historically, we know that the more the media tends to stir the pot about such issues, the less impact those issues actually have on us. It's often much ado about nothing. It's the things that come out of nowhere and blindside us that offer the real challenges.

The most successful advisors are proactive during challenging times. They get in front of topical issues and use them as a springboard to bridge to the concept of client introductions.

This isn't about trickery or tactics, but rather about leadership. If your clients are asking about topical economic issues, then you can bet they have friends and family that have similar concerns. After you have finished reassuring your client, let them know that many other clients have had similar concerns. Reiterate to the client that you will always be there if they have such concerns, again. Not only that, let them know that you will also be there if the client runs into someone who is important to them that is expressing similar concerns.

As of this writing, the topical issue is still the fallout from the market melt-down and future uncertainty combined with developments in Greece and China. Tackle these topics with your clients pro-actively, and segue the conversation into an impromptu speech that discusses introductions and referrals.

Here is one example of how to go about doing this:

In a conversation with a client during a Call Rotation process, the client says to the advisor:

"So should I be concerned about this (insert calamity here) stuff that I keep hearing about?"

To which the advisor responds:

"You know, with the cycle of 24/7 news and the volume of information on the Internet, issues like this can often get blown out of proportion. I'm not suggesting that there aren't some serious issues the government/world has to address, but the reality is that we need to tune out the noise and focus on what is relevant, and what we **can** control and plan for. The (aforementioned calamity) has become a brand unto its own and it has gone viral in the media.

"I can assure you that I watch these things very closely, and to the best of my ability, I will take appropriate steps to weather any storm that comes our way. If you would find it helpful, I would be happy to address this further. We can book a meeting if you like, and we can discuss your current plan. Is that something you would like to do?"

Depending on the degree of trust you have developed with the client, often they will say to you:

"You know what, if you aren't too concerned about it, I'm not too concerned about it."

It's at this point that you demonstrate further leadership by saying something like this:

"I became a professional advisor for this very reason. To help people face the future with anticipation rather than apprehension and to create a plan that will help them navigate through uncertain times. And, as you know, I will not only be here for you when these kinds of things make you nervous, I will also make my myself available to the people who are important to you, if indeed you encounter someone that is close to you that has similar concerns about the economy. If you are talking to someone who is concerned and they want to have a conversation with a voice of reason, let me know and I'll make myself available."

Again, it's crucial that you consistently position the concept of you speaking to friend or family member as service you are providing *for* your client, rather than as a favor you are asking *of* your client. Isn't it the right thing to do to be there for your clients, and for the people that are important to them? That's all you are saying, but you are delivering this information pro-actively, and in a way that conveys leadership.

If your intentions are true when you deliver these words, your clients will smile and say thank you. They may even send you some introductions based on your offer. Either way, the additional offer to meet with their friends and family has a secondary calming effect that your clients will appreciate.

What Triggers a Referable Moment?

We've already established that a good advisor is at their highest level of refer-ability during periods of volatility and uncertainty. Money is topical, friends and family members start to have doubts about their current advisor and all of that can lead to the client asking a friend: "Are you happy with your advisor?"

There are other referable moments, though, many of which are tied to critical events that occur in the life of a friend or family member. A divorce, an illness, the sale of a business, a death in the family, an inheritance or other "game changers" can render a current financial plan obsolete and prompt someone to seek out a trusted friend for an introduction.

Coach your clients that, when these events happen in their own lives or in the lives of the people they care about, you have a process that can help settle things down, tune out the noise, lower anxiety and create a critical path that puts things back on track.

Defining Moments

Each week I spend a considerable amount of time speaking to clients, answering their questions and suggesting possible courses of action. Without a doubt, one of the most frequent pieces of advice I offer is to *keep going*. Keep going with structured and reliable call rotations, keep sending value to your clients and prospects, keep communicating with your inside champions and/or Client Advisory Council, and keep the faith that you will realize a breakthrough.

Don't make the common mistake of assuming that, because you work with people similar to your target market, those people will want to hand you their business after a first meeting. You cannot get around the fact that you are a stranger to them. You have to take time to build familiarity and create the desire to meet with you, and the desire to know what you believe in as a person and a professional advisor.

In your written pieces, identify with your readers. If you know that most people are busy and reluctant to read a stranger's newsletter or emails, state that fact right off the top. By doing just this one thing, you have already distinguished yourself from nearly every other professional advisor.

Always try to send an interesting magazine article with your paper communications, or links to informative, interesting articles with your email communications. It will highlight as much about your client service as it does your professional services. A popular article used by several of our clients outlined the pros and cons of buying versus leasing a vehicle. While it may not seem like much, your prospect will come to understand over time that things like this separate you from other professional advisors.

Consider the effect of an article with a personal note that reads:

"I recently met with a couple and, among other things, we discussed their plans to replace their existing car. After the meeting, I searched my article library on my computer and found this item to send them. It helped these particular clients decide between leasing and buying. I hope that when the time comes, you will find it helpful as well. Keep it handy."

Other article ideas include health and fitness, vacation destinations around your area, on-line directories of local businesses and restaurants, etc. Do not fall into the trap of 'sameness', and send yet another article on mutual funds, insurance or other strictly service-related content.

Don't Stop Sending until They Ask You To

So what happens when you invite people to one of your social or open-house type events and they don't come?

You could choose to ignore them, but that won't get them 'in the door' for an initial discussion. I suggest that you follow-up with them via email or letter and tell them that you were sorry you didn't see them there, that a great time was had by all and that a lot of information was shared. Pass along a few of the questions that were asked together with the answers, and then point to your next event or remind them you are always available to meet to act as a sounding board on their investment and retirement plans.

Keep going, and ensure you continue differentiating and positioning yourself as a professional so that you will attract them when you reach them at the correct stage of readiness.

Calm, Cool and Connected: Proactive Communication

Being proactive in your communication is an important extension of your service matrix.

Communication is as big a factor for refer-ability as performance. Rates of return matter, but long-term relationships stem from trust, and trust is created by a comfort level that is supported by consistent communication.

Think of your favorite clients. They are your favorites not just because they are profitable, but also because you have great chemistry and they have virtually no hassle factor. They trust and empower you. They are aligned with you because they possess essential attitudinal qualities which include being enlightened about the realities of market cycles. They don't overreact to the highs and lows. They aren't swayed by the noise created by the media, or buy into frenzies and fears. They buy into your plan and they stick with it.

I'll come back to the metaphor that the stock markets are like the seasons. After the autumn harvest we aren't shocked that winter arrives. We know that spring will follow and then another summer and autumn. That's the way it's always been, and that's the way it will always be. The enlightened investor never says *"it's different this time."*

You probably have a handful of existing clients today who are ideal. The question is how can you best convert and create more of these ideal clients from within your client base? How can you keep them when things are chaotic? You have to coach them and lead them through a methodical communication plan, and the best time to start this is when market conditions are positive. Farmers work hard during the autumn harvest because they know winter is inevitable.

I've seen it time and time again that the advisors whose phones *don't* ring off the hook when turbulence kicks in are the advisors who pro-actively stay connected with their clients when the markets are chugging along - and therefore they don't have to reactively try to calm their clients down when things take a turn.

Furthermore, when you talk to your clients to remind them about the facts of life, you can effortlessly segue to your value proposition that also reminds them that you will make yourself available to be a sounding board for friends and family members who may be worried by the current calamity. It's worth repeating: History has shown that the best advisors are at their highest level of refer-ability when things are dicey and uncertain. Money becomes topical because fear of loss is still a bigger motivator than the possibility of a gain.

Talk to your clients and insulate them from the many factors out of your control. The more they trust you and feel comfortable with you, the more likely they will respond this way when a friend asks them if they are happy with their professional advisor:

"I've never felt better or more in control with my financial plan. My advisor helps me tune out the noise and focus on things I have control over. He has a process to ensure that I stay consistent. He doesn't 'get a hunch and buy a bunch' like old school advisors. He is my voice of reason and protects me from myself. He doesn't buy high and hope it goes higher like the herd. He buys low and hopes it doesn't go lower. I recommend him without hesitation. Would you like me to introduce you to him?"

A Simple Phrase

I never get tired of hearing clients talk about their referral process, or as is often the case, talking about their lack of a referral process. I always feel a certain sinister glee in knowing the dramatic impact I can have on an advisor's business by changing one simple thing that they are currently doing in regard to asking for referrals.

Let's assume an advisor is doing everything right with their clients. They have the clients classified, and they have an excellent service matrix that ensures that each client is getting what they deserve in relation to the revenue that they produce.

The advisor has a process for existing clients to keep them up to date and to implement the needed strategies. When the advisor meets with clients, the advisor communicates to them exactly what has been done in the past, what they are currently working on and what they could be working on in the future.

New prospective clients are treated with the utmost respect and it is clear that the initial process with them is to determine if there is a fit, and the intent is never to sell the prospect on becoming a client.

The advisor also has an excellent staff that is aware of every aspect of their client classification and knows how to pay attention to their best clients. In addition, all staff members understand F.O.R.M. and keep a report on every aspect of this crucial information for top-tier clients. The entire team recognizes 'moments of truth' within their best clients' lives and the team takes the time to honor those life circumstances as they occur, and in a meaningful way.

(As an aside: Steve Jobs had a great quote that spoke to his leadership and teamwork: "You don't hire smart people and then tell them what to do. You hire smart people so that they can tell you what to do." I'm mentioning this because it is essential that your team to see the merit in the concept of creating a playbook and doing the work to create one.)

OK, I know, I have just described the perfect practice, but, within this idyllic practice, let's now consider this advisory team's referral process. Not so much how the advisor introduces the idea of referrals, but rather the manner in which the advisor tells people to contact him.

The advisor's best clients love the advisor to pieces, and they are always excited to meet with the advisor. The clients often mention to the advisor that they have handed out the advisor's card to many of their friends over the last several months and the advisor thanks them. When the clients leave, the advisor stops to ponder, and then ponder a little more. The question that keeps arising over and over is: *"With all this goodwill, and with all these great relationships, why do I get so few calls from these otherwise perfect potential clients? My clients always mention that they know so-and-so, and he/she would be a perfect fit! And yet, the calls seldom happen."*

This is a classic lose-lose-lose situation, and it is all too common. The client feels bad about the fact that their friend never called the advisor, the friend doesn't get to meet the advisor and therefore benefit from the advisor's services, and the advisor doesn't get a great new client. So, even though it appears that this advisor is doing so much that is right, the advisor is missing out on over 90 percent of the potential referrals from those same clients that so clearly want to refer.

How easy would it be to add this simple phrase when discussing referrals with your existing clients or centers of influence rather than present the usual handful of business cards?

"I have a process. If someone expresses an interest in meeting with me, the best thing for you to do is pick up the phone, call me and make the introduction. Let your friend or family member know that I will reach out to them, and please know that I will treat them as respectfully and professionally as I do you."

Drive this with stewardship, not salesmanship. Remind them: *"Anybody you introduce to me does not need to become a client to take advantage of this service."* Based on their reaction and response move onto your process – the Why, Who and How to make an introduction to you.

By taking this one simple step, you can increase the number of referrals you receive by a factor of ten. Hey, even if it's five times, it's not like you're going to complain, right?

The One-Way Street: How to Attract Referrals from Professionals

Few professional advisors have cracked the code when it comes to consistently attracting referrals from other influencers and rainmakers who are not clients.

Now many - certainly not all – professional strategic partners are more technicians than visionaries. They often leave their clients wanting more when it comes to the big picture, market forecasts and personal investment strategy. Let's use accountants as an example, but this can apply to anyone. When a client presses their accountant to suggest a professional advisor, many are reluctant to make an endorsement. Why do you think that is? What holds them back?

It could be because they are concerned about liability issues. Perhaps they view you as a threat because they themselves aspire to add financial planning to their offerings sooner or later (or already have wealth management on-site)? Perhaps there is an issue of trust regarding your abilities and that you aren't worthy in their eyes? There are several possible reasons, but here is what I feel is the biggest issue that is undermining your refer-ability: *The accountants are uncertain as to how the endorsement will reflect back on them.*

If they are even remotely uncertain about how you will conduct yourself, or if there is a fear that the endorsement might harm their current relationship, they won't introduce a client to you. As easy as it is to wave your flag, ultimately it's just easier not to. In their minds, it isn't worth the risk.

Part of this stems from the fact that many accountants perceive professional advisors as salespeople selling products rather than consultants providing advice. In fact, that is why many accountants actually think they are doing you a favor by taking your referrals for accounting solutions without any sense that it should be a two-way street in return for investment solutions.

When you position the concept of meeting an accountant's client as a service you are providing rather than as a favor you are requesting of them, you change their perception of you. As I have repeatedly said, stewardship is far more attractive than salesmanship and is far more conducive to refer-ability, including referrals from strategic partners. If an accountant clearly knows what process you will follow when you meet with a client, and if they know that you won't try to sell their client a product or service, the mystery is gone and your refer-ability increases.

The reasons *why* many professional advisors don't get many, if any, referrals from accountants and other circles of influence are clear. Now, let's talk about *how* you can engage strategic partners and attract referrals.

The first thing I'm going to suggest you do is to ask your clients this question in your next wave of client call-rotation conversations:

"If you don't mind me asking, when you talk about me with your accountant, what do you say? How do you describe me?"

This is the best way to probe your clients to see if you have ever come up in a conversation with their accountant, and to see if your client has a clear grasp of your value proposition.

After listening to the client's response, follow-up with a personalized variation of this statement:

"The reason I ask is because I am reaching out to the accountants of my clients to arrange a time to discuss my philosophy, planning and process to ensure that we are all on the same wavelength. This is a value added service and I'm convinced that staying in closer communication with your accountant would be important. I'm wondering if you'd like me to contact your accountant so that we can touch base?"

Many clients will see the value in lighting the path for you to their accountants. Getting their permission also lends strength to your reach-out process. A variation of this can be used as part of a discussion regarding your client's estate planning lawyer, trust specialist etc.

I realize that you probably already know the names of many of your clients' accountants. The question is, have you been able to connect with them in a way that doesn't arouse any suspicions that you have a hidden agenda; that this is nothing more than a tactic to make more sales? Your approach has to be professional, forthright, transparent and, most of all, rooted in value and service.

Once you've gathered the names and numbers of your clients' accountants, look for commonalities and cross reference with your existing relationships. Then begin the process of reaching out to them.

When you make contact, explain the reason you are calling. It will generally come down to one of two motivations. If you have never met, but you have a mutual client, you'd like to discuss your financial strategy and financial outlook to be sure that you are both in sync with each other. If you have an existing one-way-street type relationship with accountant, you are calling to discuss ways that you can strengthen your relationship. Keep in mind the unspoken concerns and resistances that revolve around the questions they will ask themselves: *"What's in it for me?"* and *"What's the risk?"*

In response to your offer to meet with them they will either accept your invite, decline, or ask you to elaborate on the phone. While it's tempting to do an abbreviated meeting over the phone, I would suggest you resist the urge and insist that you meet. A breakfast or lunch meeting, or a sit-down in their boardroom, is ideal.

The following strategy is drawn from our consulting program for professional advisors. This is a guideline, a skeleton to build on, and I'm asking you to tailor it to suit your own approach and personality. The key is to get busy, start engaging in the process and refine it as you go.

As I often say, done is better than perfect. Just get it done and communicate this message to as many accountants as you can. I'm not going to suggest that this will work every time – it won't. When it comes to persuasion and the communication of a concept, you have to keep in mind that you can't want it more than the listener does. This process is like sifting for gold. You may have to move a ton of dirt to find an ounce of gold.

In some cases, you'll have people who respond favorably and then do nothing and others who don't see the merit and decline. This process will help you determine if there is good mutual chemistry and fit, so that you can temper your expectations accordingly. That said, if you follow this process closely, you will find that it is *universal*. Not only can this work effectively with accountants but also for lawyers, HR staff and other professional influencers who can become rainmakers for you.

If strategic partners realize that they can trust you to make them look good and to essentially relieve them of some burdens, your refer-ability will go through the roof and your phone will ring consistently. All it takes is for a couple of their clients to get back to them saying *"the best thing I did was talk to your advisor."* Validation like that will contrast you favorably against other advisors and generate a high level of self-motivation among the professionals you approach, and those essential ingredients will open the referral floodgates.

The following is a format I would encourage you to follow. It doesn't just tell about your process, it shows you have and use one and it and contrasts you to those swimming in the pool-of-sameness:

Step 1 – Have a printed agenda to outline your key points, to give you a track to follow and to convey clearly that you follow a methodical process. Have the agenda in a leather portfolio along with a pen and notepad so that the accountant can take notes. This also serves as a tangible leave-behind that anchors them to your professionalism.

Step 2 – Connect with the Accountant and discuss your Three Ps (Philosophy, Planning and Process) as they relate to the client, and perhaps embed your trailer. Probe for insight and feedback throughout the meeting. Explain your process and commitment to consistency and best practices.

Step 3 – Ask for their Opinion to find out what is important to them, or, when it comes to investment planning, to describe their investment philosophy and to what extent they discuss investment planning, insurance and other wealth management solutions.

Step 4 – Transition the conversation to explain that you have several value-added services that your clients find to be of benefit, including the fact that you make yourself available to act as a sounding board for friends and family members. The accountant you are talking to may already have an advisor or two that they currently endorse to their clients. At this point you are contrasting your approach to the current advisor's to break the status quo and encourage the accountant to consider you as an option. Position this as part of your process.

Step 5 – Explain WHY you do this by saying: *Recently, in light of this market* (or whatever the current focus is), *I've been making myself available to act as a sounding board for friends and family members of my clients as well as clients of like-minded accountants with whom I have a relationship.*

Step 6 – Explain that the people you meet do not need to become a client to take advantage of this service. You do it because of the fulfillment that comes from helping people make informed decisions.

Step 7 – Stress how you realize that this has to be a good use of the individual's time. Use the words 'process' and 'service' continually and explain what happens during the sounding board session. One good phrase is this: *"I don't want to claim that miracles will occur, but one of two things will happen when I meet with one of your clients, either I will validate that their current approach is fundamentally solid, or I will reveal a few minor flaws that they may want to consider adjusting. After all, minor adjustments can often lead to major improvements down the road."*

Step 8 – Explain WHO you do this for. Say that you occasionally meet people who you hit it off with and you may decide to work together – explain who those people are using your AAA ideal client profile, based on Assets and needs fitting your areas of expertise, Attitudes being complementary and Advocacy traits, illustrating that clients aren't buying something from you, they are buying into something with you.

Step 9 – Be forthright in terms of defining your points of difference. While many advisors are generalists trying to be all things to all people, you are a specialist striving to be all things to some people.

Step 10 – Project scarcity by explaining that if someone presses you to become a client but doesn't meet your profile you won't bring them on as a client. Explain that, while some advisors will work with anyone and try to see how big they can build their business, you prefer to focus on how small you can stay to ensure consistent service.

Step 11 – Explain HOW to get the wheels in motion should a situation present itself by suggesting the accountant contact you directly to make the introduction.

Step 12 – Be crystal clear that you will ensure that the client will view meeting with you as being a great investment of their time and that the accountant can hold you accountable that you will afford his or her client the same degree of professionalism and confidentiality that you provide your clients.

Step 13 – Mention that this will be a two-way street. You'd like to be able to follow the same process when it comes to introducing your clients to the accountant should the situation arise.

Step 14 – Be Patient. Many accountants and other professionals are hyper-cautious and you will need to nurture the relationship methodically to move from intent to actual consent. Many advisors get frustrated because accountants say all the right things in the beginning, but then their intent diminishes and their fears creep back in. Patience is needed to allay that fear.

There are some professional advisors who have taken this process to a completely new level. When they onboard a new client, they are crystal clear about their rules of engagement. They say to the new client:

"One of the steps in my process is that once a year you, your accountant and I will be getting together for lunch. You will be buying an hour of her time. I will be buying a great lunch and together we will tune out the world and make sure we are all aligned."

This is not positioned as a question. It is part of the process. You can imagine how many referrals they get and how they never have a client calling saying "My accountant just contacted me and questioned how much I'm paying you."

Visit **www.TheAdvisorPlaybook.com** for access
to the Playbook Implementation Program

Section 6: The Advisor of the Future

Integrating it All

The secret of your future is hidden in your daily routine - Mike Murdock

---

LinkedIn Essentials

Now that you've taken the stewardship over salesmanship model onboard and are a serious developer of your personal brand, you may be wondering to what degree social networking and the on-line ecosystem can affect your strategy and overall business development efforts.

Let's be candid: Most of what's available to you is social 'not-working'. For a big business or for a celebrity, Twitter, Facebook and similar services can be of value due to their reach. For a professional advisor who is trying to be found by prospective clients, rather than looking like he or she is trying to headhunt new clients, it's a different story. The bottom line is this: I know many top-caliber advisors who never go near social media.

LinkedIn, however, can be a different story. It can let you stay in touch, stir the pot and be proactive and accessible. Done properly and consistently, this solution can assist you in competitor-proofing clients. It can make it easy for clients to introduce you in a way that allows the people they know to get to know *you* before the first real contact. I don't profess to be an expert in the area and I know there are many out there who are, like Pat Woerfel at First Trust and Stephen Boswell at The Oechsli Institute, to name just two. I personally and professionally use LinkedIn extensively and it continues to surprise me. It gains traction month after month. It's a substantial community with new people constantly joining and raising a hand to opt in.

Searchability – The Art of Being Found

Your LinkedIn profile and the traffic you drive to it can have a profound impact on your search engine optimization strategy. Think about it. Your client puts you on the radar of a friend, colleague or business associate. That person goes back to his or her desk – or even right to their smart phone – and does a Google search on you. It takes them directly to your LinkedIn profile. Instantly, you have a captive audience and you can activate the relationship cycle.

The validation, contrast and predisposition I've been talking about can be amplified instantly with a good profile. Confucius advised us about a journey of a thousand miles, and this is that first step.

Your profile is your store-front, for lack of a better term. Is it instantly inviting, to the point and does it have curb appeal? It should emphasize the person, the practice and the process without jargon and data-dumping. So, have some sizzle, get to the point and leave them wanting more.

How do you do that? Use your value proposition to address these four key points:

1. **Who is your ideal client?**
2. **What do they want from you?**
3. **How do you get them there?**
4. **Refer to it as process and give it a name.**

It would be a good idea to invest the time, money and effort to create a brief video with your trailer from the first section; a three-minute video overview of your philosophy, planning strategy and process. The beauty of a video is that it can be embedded into your website and be featured in your introductory package, CD or linked to your email, as well.

Stirring the Pot is Different than Stalking

LinkedIn is an excellent tool to help encourage introductions to others but it can be a little creepy when someone you don't know makes observations about you that were clearly acquired through an Internet search. The key is to stay congruent with stewardship so that you don't look sales-y and needy. Many advisors drive it with the *Law of Reciprocity*. They know the world is round and they are constantly inviting people in their networks with statements like:

"Let me know if there is anyone in my network you would like me to introduce to you."

Or

"Tell me how you would like me to describe you when I get the opportunity to introduce you."

Over time, this triggers a reciprocal action and you can go to your value proposition and connect the dots for them as they start making introductions for you.

If someone in a connected network stands out and you'd like to prompt an introduction, be low-key and subtle. Make reference to the person, how they know each other and inquire as to whether or not they'd be interested in mentioning some of your content, such as a white-paper or recorded presentation.

Consistently use specifics over generalities when mentioning your ideal client. Telling someone you are not all things to all people and reinforcing that with your value proposition and ideal client profile helps you project scarcity, specificity and professionalism.

The importance of emphasizing both your chemistry and your credentials when networking needs to be stressed. Skills and solutions like yours are everywhere, but trusting relationships are rare. Make sure you delay gratification, be patient and don't be too pushy (or creepy) in your intel-gathering and initial contact. The tools within LinkedIn, let alone on other sites, that help you get to know something about people is staggering (and, again, a bit creepy). Be careful to walk the line professionally. Talk about specific people, commonalities and interesting aspects of their profile. Schools, interests and F.O.R.M.-related information that you uncover can be an excellent lead-in.

As in all target marketing, the key is patience, consistency and professionalism. Let your efforts build upon themselves over time and your activity will lead to productivity.

As always, use the 80/20 rule to allocate your time. Empower your staff to be active on your LinkedIn profile acknowledging birthdays, milestones, commentary and other noteworthy issues on behalf of your team. You don't have to spend an hour a day yourself on LinkedIn, and between you and your team, you can build serious momentum that ultimately leads to measurable results.

I have to tell you, though, how this semi-backfired on me, once. I was presenting to a large group and I invited them to join my LinkedIn network. Someone in the front row took out his phone and proceeded to send an invite. Which I accepted, while still presenting.

It was a team member back in the office who happened to be on my network. The seminar attendee called me on it right then and there. We had a good laugh but I then reminded everyone about the power of teamwork and delegation. Call it spin and quick thinking but, in truth, our team is bought into the cause.

How to Develop a Website and Online Marketing Strategy

From a business development perspective, your website can become an essential and dependable 24/7 driver for you.

Of all the benefits that today's savvy advisors are achieving with their websites and on-line communications, the most important is in making it effortless for clients to introduce friends, family members and business associates.

Your web-presence can enhance your referrals and act as an approachable route for communication, not just for your existing clients, but for their statistical circle of 52 friends and family.

The Rule of 52

The beauty of an effective on-line strategy is that you are providing an accessible and professional bridge between you and the people your clients can influence. We've talked about the Rule of 52 in passing. Let's dig deeper into why it can be potent, and how to approach it.

The Rule of 52 suggests that every client has their own inner circle of about 52 friends and family members. If you currently have 300 clients, use the 80/20 rule and look at how many elite clients you have; roughly 60. Now, apply 80/20 to that 60. That gives you something like 15 top-of-the-top clients. Multiply that 15 by 52. You have a super-high-quality target-market universe of about 780 people.

How do you reach them?

In this era, prospective clients want to get to know you before they meet you. A good website can help people develop a virtual connection with you on their own terms and the relationship can proceed from there. Your goal is to teach your clients to use your website as your virtual business card and, in the process, make it an indispensable utility to everyone.

The key lies in how your clients currently perceive your website. Do they think of it as a billboard that says "Here I Am"? Or do they think of it as a vibrant resource? All of your promotional efforts trigger either a "me too" that people connect with or a "so what" that they dismiss. If the first impression from your website is that of selling investments, people will tune you out and never return. If, on the other hand, people see that you have developed a reputation for engagement and education, you drastically change the signal-to-noise ratio and in the process become more referable.

This has never been more important than right now. Money and all things related to the markets are incredibly topical. Couple that with the fact that people have more apprehension for the future than anticipation. That anxiety, along with the degree of doubt that a lot of people have for their current financial provider, can be an opportunity for you to position yourself as the go-to advisor.

From Integration to Convergence

Think of your website as an information hub.

When clients realize that you don't try to sell to people but rather inform them, they know that they can wave your flag without fear. To complement this you should create a habitual approach to providing market commentary, insights and updates and feed it into your site on consistent basis. Your E-newsletter (one of the most effective tools available to you) can integrate with your social media efforts and feed into your website. It might sound like work, but there are templates and automated procedures that can make it easy, and keep you compliant along the way.

If you want to take this seriously, and I'd be surprised if you weren't, do as I suggested earlier and have a professional video made of your trailer, and put it everywhere: Websites, LinkedIn, *everywhere*.

One of the most remarkable aspects of social media is seamless convergence. All of your micro-blogging efforts and other postings can be efficiently integrated to give you maximum reach with minimal effort. I don't want to oversimplify things because social media requires a balance of knowledge and effort, but if you are a serious student, learning as you go, and you set realistic expectations, you will incrementally gather momentum and get into a groove.

With a little research and some trial and error, you can launch a simple "surface" campaign and run it yourself at a cost of about an hour a day. Again, contrary to the old cliché, time is not money. Time is more valuable and the best way to ensure a solid ROI is to develop a skill set and be consistent and patient.

If you want to get "serious", I suggest you interview some consulting firms who specialize in social media support. But don't out-source the work entirely. Instead, work alongside the firm so that you can hold them accountable and learn valuable skills that will serve you going forward.

Become a Content Machine

The advisors who generate momentum on-line are those who are consistent and frequent in their content and updates.

Sporadic efforts don't compound. Weekly, bi-weekly or monthly updates that are predictable, brief and actionable become familiar and people look forward to receiving them. That said, you do have to temper your expectations and realize it requires time to reach fruition. This is a "building exercise" that differentiates you from all the dabbling "one-and-done" advisors who try an on-line approach and give up soon after.

I'm working with a number of advisors who are creating White Papers and other content-marketing tools that they can use as part of their calls to action in their business development activities. Rather than asking prospective clients to "call to receive a complimentary review of your portfolio", you want them to ask for something they can visualize and perceive as having value instead of being sales-centered. When you ask people to "call to receive my White Paper that outlines The Top 10 Mistakes Investors Make" you position yourself as an expert while sifting prospects from suspects. Your call to action acts as a bridge and a Trojan horse. It also gives you something to point to in follow-up efforts down the road.

The Trojan Horse

As I mentioned, the most powerful driver that can build interest and predisposition among your clients and MVPs is an ongoing E-newsletter.

A tip of the week or weekly blog post has proven to be effective at not only keeping clients connected to you (and competitor-proof) but also for dripping on prospective clients. Follow these three simple rules:

1. Be consistent (weekly, bi-weekly or monthly) and archive all posts on your website.

2. Invite your clients to forward your weekly E-newsletter to friends.

3. Have an opt-in feature that allows people to subscribe.

The Multimedia Advisor: How to Make It Easy For People to Refer You

When it comes to new client acquisition, one of the most powerful things you can do is create tools that enable your clients to effortlessly introduce you to their friends, while at the same time making it easy for those friends to develop a relationship before they ever have to meet with you. The virtual world can be an excellent place to do just that.

Your clients can have immense persuasive impact on the people they know, but it often takes time between the moment a prospect becomes aware of you and the moment they feel compelled to take action. It would be nice if a friend of a client instantly acted on an endorsement of you, but high-net-worth people are busy, skeptical and are conditioned to conduct at least some due diligence before making a meaningful change in their approach. Don't get me wrong, affluent people want to believe that there are better alternatives to the status quo, but experience has taught them to be disbelieving.

All your prospective clients have a relationship with a current financial services provider, at least on some level. There is a good chance that they have an adequate relationship, but that they are far from dazzled. There is even a good chance that those prospects have switched from one provider to another in the past and that previous transition was anticlimactic. If their current advisor over-promised to close the client and under-delivered once they were on board, expectations were set but not met, let alone exceeded. This means that while they may be indifferent or even disillusioned with their current provider, they also may lack any motivation to switch because of a lack of confidence that you will be an upgrade.

Building your Online You

With the foregoing in mind, your job is to create some mind-share and familiarity with those prospects and slowly position yourself as a favorable alternative. This can take time.

This mind-share building process builds their awareness for you, and eventually a predisposition to meet you, because your value is contrasted favorably to that of their current provider. The steps in the Relationship Cycle progress as follows:

- *Client Makes an Endorsement* – You are officially on a friend or family member's radar.

- ***Friend Builds Awareness for You*** – They start evaluating you from a distance by checking you out on-line.

- ***They Develop an Interest in You*** – Your messaging and branding strategy resonates with them.

- ***They Develop Trust for You*** – They see the value in meeting you.

- ***They Empower You*** – You validate their feelings and their intent shifts to consent.

- ***They Endorse You*** – They eventually introduce a friend to you and it comes full circle.

One of the best ways to put the odds in your favor and fast-track the process is to create content and virtual deliverables that enable a client to subtly plant the seed in a friend's mind, so that friend can begin to evaluate you on his or her own terms.

Social networking, weekly factoids, white papers and other content have been proven to be surefire ways – if done properly – to act as a bridge between a client and a friend. Why not consider taking it a step further? How about creating a brief and informative multimedia suite of self-promoting tools that can dynamically communicate your value?

There are a handful of top professional advisors who have created audio tools in the form of recorded seminars, podcasts and other resources offered to clients as value-adds and archived on websites for prospects to access and subscribe to. Some advisors have created brief video infomercials to outline their value proposition and enable prospects to make a virtual connection, put a face and voice to the name and move awareness to interest a little more quickly.

Be warned: These videos can't be sales-oriented elevator speeches. Your goal, as always, is to position yourself as an expert, not to be perceived as a salesperson. Integrate your value proposition and your overall branding strategy; make sure you have convergence of message. You want your prospective clients to realize quickly that you aren't trying to sell them something. You are trying to teach them something and communicate value that speaks to them. Follow this simple formula when creating your own video, and refer constantly to your trailer:

1. A Hook that Resonates – You aren't explaining who you are or what you do early in the video. You want to address a problem that speaks to the prospect. The hook is about them and their issues, not about your skills, services or solutions.

"Are you a business owner that is concerned about your Family Legacy and the smooth transition from one generation to the next?"

2. I'm a Specialist, Not a Generalist – Once you have their attention with good hook, tell them how you have solved this problem for others in the past and that this is your area of expertise.

"There are several pieces to the family legacy process and we've been putting those pieces together for our clients for over 15 years."

3. I Have a Purpose – Explain your "why": Why you became a professional advisor and why you chose this approach.

"I became a professional advisor to help business owners make informed decisions and help them face the future with anticipation instead of apprehension. It's fulfilling to help people tune out the noise and deploy a plan that's tailored to their personal situation and objectives."

4. I Have a Process – Your business can be abstract, so remove the mystery and define your process using a catchy caption that conveys strength and is immediately understood and valued.

"We advise our clients through the sequential deployment of our Family Legacy Process."

This is just one generic version of countless promotional branding messages that have proven to instantly resonate with prospective clients within a specific target market.

When you complement this messaging with a strong, purposeful story, you activate the mind-share process and make contrasting you favorably to their current provider very predictable. Then, if you use the DRIP process on prospects with additional value, ideally using an opt-in strategy, you start creating a nagging feeling in their minds that they have to meet you in person.

Awareness leads to interest which leads to trust which leads to empowerment and eventually to an endorsement. Use a process and the Relationship Cycle will work for you over and over again.

The Bridge to Client Acquisition

One of the most important components of any classic marketing strategy is the call to action. While you need a good hook to get the prospect's attention and you need a strong core message to build his or her interest, at some point you have to ask them to take action.

It's not much different in a referral scenario, either. Your best client could be having a conversation with a friend or family member and the topic of money comes up. The friend then says to your client, *"Are you happy with your professional advisor?"* How does your client respond? What action do they tell their friend to take? The same holds true with an accountant or other strategic partner you collaborate with. What action do you tell them to take when an opportunity to introduce you presents itself?

Many professional advisors use a similar and worn out call to action in their marketing efforts. Whether it's at seminars, campaigns, or on the phone, most advisors invite people to contact them for a "complimentary review of their portfolio" or a "second opinion".

I'm not suggesting that a portfolio review for the purposes of a second opinion is a bad idea, but the key is on how prospects *interpret* that call to action. It involves a commitment to meet you and, as easy as that is to do, it's always easier not to. Furthermore, variations of this call to action have been used over the years by countless marketers, and frankly people see right through it as a tactic to get you in a room to put the pressure on to close the deal.

Bottom line, it's falling on deaf ears.

One of the most effective ways to sift prospects from suspects and get them to contact you is to deploy a permission marketing approach such as I've touched on repeatedly. This means that you change the call to action from asking them to meet you personally to asking them to request some content from you on-line. They can begin a relationship with you without actually meeting you at first.

If you offer an executive summary of a seminar topic you presented on, or if you offer a white paper, report or Top 10 List outlining a theme that your prospect can relate to, you are making it easier to contact you via requesting this content. This acts as a bridge for them cross without having to commit to meeting you just yet. When they contact you, they are raising their hands and essentially saying *"Tell me more - I'm interested. But you are going to have to earn the right to meet me."*

Content takes the abstract nature of what you do and transforms it into something much easier to conceptualize. Think about how someone would envision the concept of a piece of content versus the invitation to meet for a second opinion. They can imagine themselves holding this content in their hands and learning about your message as well as the messenger.

This content is not a brochure, prospectus or product spotlight. It is your (compliance approved) interpretation of mistakes people make, or strategies someone can act on. It's a stepping-stone; a bridge to you.

Ideally, the message speaks directly to your target audience and complements your value proposition. Note that it doesn't have to be core-services-specific. For example, if you target business owners, you can speak to common myths about affluent business owners as described in Tom Stanley's great book *The Millionaire Next Door*. If you target the newly retired, you can speak to the common mistakes the soon-to-be-retired make just prior to their transition.

Content Makes You Referable

The biggest benefit of creating content is that you make it easier for clients and strategic partners to refer people to you. Rather than a call to action that begs people to "Have Your Friend Call Me", tell people this:

"If someone ever asks you about me, or you feel compelled to introduce someone to me, call me or shoot me an email and I will forward my white paper on 'The Top 10 Components to a Solid Financial Plan'. If nothing else, this will help them tune out the noise and focus on what really matters when it comes to navigating these turbulent market conditions."

Your clients and partners can conceptualize this and it's easy for them to relay and describe it to someone else. After you've told them about your content and invited them to use it as a bridge to introduce people to you, complement it with this value proposition to galvanize their trust in you:

"As you know, there are two types of professional advisors out there. There are salespeople who ask you to buy investments, and there are consultants who ask you to buy into a process and a meaningful relationship. I provide content like this to help people make informed decisions and face the future with anticipation rather than apprehension."

The DRIP Process: Friction-Free Client Acquisition

Without leaving the digital world entirely, I want to return most of the focus to the analogue.

I'll be elaborating on the importance of identifying an inside champion and developing an insider's reputation, but you will also want to reach out to your MVPs and begin positioning yourself as No. 2; creating that nagging feeling in clients' minds that they are currently with the wrong advisor and should consider how much better-served they would be in a relationship with you.

At the risk of oversimplifying the process, professional prospecting is about being consistent, persistent and respectful. Keep in mind that you want prospects to contrast you favorably to their current advisors, which takes time. This approach combines the mindset of a professional: It includes diligence and patience. I frame this approach with the acronym DRIP.

Once you begin the process, subscribe to the mantra that says *you have to drip on prospects until they buy or die.* Again, you aren't asking them to buy investments, you are asking them to *buy into* your professionalism and your process. It does take time - sometimes a year or more - but with this approach your efforts compound, and in time your momentum will take on a life of its own and achieve critical mass.

The D in Drip stands for DISCIPLINE.

Like anything, as easy as this is, ultimately it's easier not to do. A lot of advisors will get excited about this approach and then realize that it looks a lot like work.

Discipline applies to all aspects of the process. You have to delay gratification and dig deep to gather the knowledge capital necessary to be attractive to prospective clients in your target market. You also have to be excited and passionate about the target market. As the saying goes, in order to be convincing, you have to be convinced. Fortunately we have search engines that can help you track down any information you need.

When you approach your inside champion to ask for his or her guidance, you are essentially using a variation of permission marketing which creates a deeper level of chemistry, respect and reciprocity. Most people you approach will gladly share more information than you could ever need. I remember one scenario in which the advisor's inside champion offered to help the advisor organize a variation of a client advisory council. The inside champion filled the room with entrepreneurial friends of his to help the advisor get inside the heads of a typical self-made successful entrepreneur.

The second factor related to discipline is that, as you start reaching out to other prospective clients in the sector, you have to resign yourself to patience. As with any process where you are trying to build a relationship first and do business second, it takes a little time. Keep your ultimate objective in mind. Every person you contact will already have a professional advisor. There is a stage of readiness at which the prospective client will come to his or her own conclusion that switching to you makes absolute sense.

The third aspect of discipline is to delay gratification in your calls to action. Don't rush to ask prospects to meet with you, let alone buy something from you. Instead, offer them the opportunity to request information such as a white paper. They are expecting to be sold by you. When you don't meet that expectation, you stand out from the pack. By using content marketing, their positive responses give you permission to go deeper and build a relationship and trust early on.

This delayed approach requires discipline but has been proven to be effective at creating a positive first impression, and how you start a relationship has so much impact on how it will unfold over the long term.

The R in Drip stands for RESPECT.

In this process you have to interact respectfully, not look needy and not potentially cause any collateral damage to your existing relationship, let alone to the sector itself. This is why I ask you to resist cold calling in the classic sense where you have a dialing-for-dollars mindset. Yes, you want to smile and dial, but you aren't connecting to have them buy something, you want them to buy into your story. If you call up with a data-dumping sales pitch and elevator speech, you are chasing the person, and what you chase will often elude you. When you make contact with a compelling hook and promise statement that explains why you are working with this specific sector, and you offer up information and a sounding board session rather than an offer to sell something, you are attracting the prospective client.

Again, everything you say is either a 'me too' or a 'so what'. Show respect throughout the process.

The I in DRIP stands for INFORM.

You have to be informative, yet have some personality as well. Rehearse, Refine and Reflect on all of your scripting.

Is it compelling? To paraphrase David Ogilvie, you can't bore someone into taking action. Your events and lunch-and-learns have to be unique and must have a hook that resonates with the target audience. You have to build chemistry with prospective clients.

Look at the word inform – the last four letters speak to F.O.R.M. – your conversations have to be balanced. Ask questions about their family, occupation and recreational interests, not just about their money.

As an example, you might be talking to a prospective client and you ask him what his kids are into. He tells you that his 10-year-old is into hockey. You mention that your own 10-year-old is also a hockey nut and the next thing you know, you are talking about hockey for 20 minutes. You have made a deeper connection. You aren't just trying to be interesting, you are interested.

Be Socratic. Ask questions. Every answer gives you permission to go deeper.

And, finally:

The P in DRIP stands for PERSIST.

You have to be persistent. This process takes time. It's not unusual to need seven drips on a prospective client before he or she will agree to meet with you. As the old saying goes, water dripping on a stone will eventually leave a mark. With every drip you are building contrast with the prospective client's current advisor and distancing yourself from anyone else who is dabbling and trying to get them as a client, too.

Have a process to invest every drip into the rest of the relationship. A relationship journal within your CRM will help you keep track and convert all the knowledge you glean from every encounter into an invaluable intellectual property.

I don't want to oversimplify this approach; this is just an overview and framework, but if you follow it you will realize that Margaret Thatcher was right when she said, "It's good be a starter but you have to be a sticker too. It's easy enough to start a job, but it's harder to see it through."

Bringing it All Together

James Allen, author of many great books including *As a Man Thinketh*, had several memorable quotes including, "Circumstances don't make the man; they reveal him."

Circumstances in the financial services industry over the last few years have revealed that trust between many affluent clients and their professional advisors has been adversely impacted, and in some cases shattered. Coupled with increased commoditization and the advent of robo-advisors, the result is many high net-worth clients who are disillusioned with their current advisor or are attempting a DIY approach. They are open to considering their options, but they haven't made a switch because, in their view, a superior option hasn't come along.

In light of this, there has never been a better time to implement a professional target marketing strategy that differentiates you from the pack and elevates your image and branding in the marketplace.

While the following is a compendium of an in-depth process, the spine of this strategy stems directly from the Pareto System coaching and consulting program and has been proven to not only be effective at consistently attracting good prospective clients but it is also philosophically consistent with our stewardship over salesmanship model.

This process ties together many of the concepts and strategies introduced earlier in this book:

1. **Identify your MVPs** – Who are your Most Valued Prospects?

2. **Create an Inside Champion** – Someone who can help you become a trusted guru within the target market.

3. **Develop an Insider's Reputation** – Acquire essential knowledge to be compelling to prospective clients within the target market.

4. **Deploy a Process** – To connect with the target market and create a nagging feeling they are currently with the wrong advisor.

5. **Position Yourself as No. 2** – Help your MVPs contrast you favorably and become more acutely aware of the doubts they have about their current advisor.

6. **Be Consistent and Persistent** – Use knowledge-based communications and permission marketing to make it easy for MVPs to connect with you.

Allow me to begin by taking one step back. It is essential that you get *focused* and establish your MVPs before you get started. The friends and family members of your clients are your best MVPs and the clients of your strategic partners are a close second. Assuming you have done a good job maximizing your existing client relationships and you have professionally engaged strategic influencers such as accountants and lawyers, and you still find yourself with some time to deploy a pure prospecting campaign, you can apply this process.

An important first step at the outset is to understand the difference between broadcasting and narrow-casting, and why you want the second and not the first.

Broadcasting

Broadcasting consists of classic marketing concepts such as direct mail, cold calling, newspaper ads, trade shows, etc. It's "spray and pray" marketing and it's often about as effective as cutting down a tree with a hammer.

Narrow-casting

Narrow-casting, on the other hand, is a sharp ax. You pin-point a specific geographic, demographic or socioeconomic sector in your marketplace and you methodically and relentlessly turn it upside down. Broadcasting is a mile wide and an inch deep. Narrow-casting enables you to go deep and literally turn a target market into an impenetrable proprietary asset that your competitors will never crack.

Finding an Inside Champion

So how do you identify a target market to narrow-cast? Start by looking at your favorite clients and identify an *Inside Champion*.

Look at what your favorite clients do for a living. I know of a professional advisor who had a great client who was an audiologist. I suggested that he contact the client and ask him out to lunch. At the meeting the advisor said, *"Look, I really enjoy our relationship and frankly I'm fascinated with what you do. I want to become a specialist in your field rather than a generalist trying to be all things to all people. Tell me, what do I need to know, what do I need to read and where do I need to go to be a specialist to people just like you?"*

The lunch meeting lasted a couple of hours. The client did a majority of the talking, first by applauding the advisor for his initiative, and then went on to counsel him on what it would take to be a specialist to Audiologists. The rest, as they say, is history. A few years later, and after a lot of effort and homework, this advisor pretty much owns that space.

Earning a Reputation

The aforementioned advisor, with the help of the inside champion, began the process of developing an *Insider's Reputation*. He developed the knowledge, insight and visibility that allowed him to connect and relate with his target audience in a way that made him compelling and unique.

There are no limits. I've seen an advisor who owned a BMW motorcycle accidentally uncover the fact one of his best clients also owned a BMW motorbike. After making the connection that owners of BMW motorcycles are usually somewhat affluent, he approached the local dealer to see if he would sponsor and help promote a fund-raising ride for the local children's hospital. That was just the beginning to what has become an incredible target marketing effort.

I've seen seasoned advisors establish target markets with orthodontists and other professional sectors within the health and wellness community, all stemming from one existing relationship. I've seen newer advisors establish target markets with franchise owners and other entrepreneurs. You can pretty much name it. From airline pilots to zoologists, advisors have built target markets based on a diverse array of affinity groups.

To this day, one of my favorite examples is that of an advisor whose assistant's dairy farmer father became a client. He quickly developed an incredible relationship with the advisor. That one relationship, along with some sustained effort, led to dozens of new clients in the dairy industry, and (talk about an insider's reputation) this advisor went to county fairs, wrote financial planning articles in dairy trade publications and today is the go-to guy for dairy farmers in his area. He lived by the mantra that you have to pull in the direction that people are already pushing you.

That is where momentum develops.

Visit **www.TheAdvisorPlaybook.com** for access

to the Playbook Implementation Program

Section 7: The Next Chapter

Done is Better Than Perfect

*Knowledge is learning something every day. Wisdom is
letting go of something every day* – Zen aphorism

Be Positioned for Anything

Being well-positioned requires knowing where you are and where you're headed. If your goals are clear, as are your rules of engagement, and you've put together a plan on a panoramic and personal level using the W5 process and S.T.A.R., you are ready to start fine-tuning your future and rise to the next level.

I speak with literally hundreds of professional advisors each year and I hear first-hand what they're hoping to achieve in the future. Some goals are quite common, while others are counter-intuitive. On any given day I will speak to an advisor who aspires to more and wants to grow his or her business, and then on the next call I will speak to another advisor who strives for contentment and wants to simplify his or her life.

At the 30,000-foot perspective, on virtually every call I can categorize each advisor into one or more of these three areas:

Explore - The advisor wants to conduct a gap analysis to identify untapped opportunities and overlooked vulnerabilities.

Evolve - The advisor wants to break out of the status quo and make the refinements necessary to get to the next level of efficiency and profitability.

Expand - The advisor wants to develop personally and professionally to achieve greater fulfillment and predictability on a daily basis.

You can then slice those three categories into individual needs, and ten of them are most prevalent among advisors who are at the top of their fields. When I drill down on these calls and uncover the core motivators, the following are the most common goals advisors share:

The Top Ten Goals of Elite Advisors

To right-size their business to restore liberation and order to their lives as they focus on their best clients.

To transition to a fee-based model in a professional manner, so that clients focus on what the advisor is worth rather than what he or she costs.

To align with another advisor to create scale, efficiency and a 1+1=3 environment that is more profitable and fulfilling – or work with a protégé to map out a succession.

To be better prepared for market volatility to ensure they thrive rather than just survive in any market conditions.

To buy a business from a retiring advisor and predictably integrate it into their existing business.

To switch to a different firm where the culture and core philosophy are complementary to the advisor's.

To sell their business for maximum profit by amplifying the proprietary assets beyond just the 'Trailing 12'.

To create the organization and structure needed to unlock efficiency and profitability.

To increase high-level client acquisition by attracting like a consultant, rather than chasing like a salesperson.

To develop outstanding branding so that the advisor is perceived and described as a professional with a process.

On the route to accomplishing all the above, there are two golden rules top achievers never break:

1. They don't wing it.

2. They don't wait for conditions to be perfect.

The most enlightened advisors understand the balance between planning and taking action with a sense of urgency. Substantial goals are achieved by design, not by chance.

When an advisor comes to us with a vision for how they want their business and life to look in the future, the key mindset we want to support is that of getting out in front of an issue and pro-actively driving it with a methodical and sequential plan.

Of course, that's a lot easier to talk about than it is to actually do, but time and time again I see, firsthand, how success is achieved by letting disciplines compound over time. I also see the impact of neglect. If we neglect the things we should be doing, it compounds and takes us further away from our goals.

If you have a vision for how you would like your life and business to look in the next 12 months, it is essential that you break down the necessary actions and chip away at it over time. This puts you on a trajectory that enables you to make mid-course corrections quickly so that you don't drift off track.

Successful advisors with serious mileage and experience will tell you that meaningful change takes longer, requires more resources, and is more difficult to execute than expected. Just as a savvy investor knows that it's dangerous to think *"It's different this time"*, the advisor who aspires for bigger and better things has to temper their optimism and know that external dependencies may not always cooperate.

Overcoming that adversity makes the achievement that much more meaningful.

If it is to be it is up to me!

Those are quite possibly the ten most powerful two-letter words ever put together in one sentence. It is what separates the best advisors from the rest. They take action, and they take responsibility for their outcome. They don't blame conditions and adversity or wish *things* were better. They strive to *become* better.

The secret of getting ahead is getting started – Mark Twain

Connecting With Clients on a Different Level

Not everything needs to be grim determination in the face of adversity, though. Connecting with community-centric communication is also a potent and satisfying tool. It is a complement to your branding strategy that emphasizes your purpose and fulfillment.

At a recent workshop I was conducting for financial advisors, I talked about the importance of an advisor injecting some personality into his or her client-communications strategy. It's one thing to think of your business as an actual business, but I'd also like you to think of it as a community that your clients want to belong to. Building long-term client relationships isn't just about the returns you help them achieve, it's also about how being your client makes them feel. The better they feel about your community, the more likely they will stay loyal and introduce a friend or family member to you.

A great idea that came out of that workshop was this: Have each advisor and support staffer at your business bring in a picture of their family. Create a collage of the pictures in a large frame and display it in the reception area. Other advisors have instituted a variation of this by putting family pictures, photos of team initiatives such as fund raisers and other charitable events in a photo album and leaving it on the coffee table in the client waiting area. In every case, advisors who have done this talk about how favorably people respond. Prospective clients aspire to belong to the community, clients feel good about belonging and your staffers love the vibe this concept creates in the office.

Take this concept of creating a feeling of community beyond the office.

I know a professional advisor who sponsored a young swimming sensation from a financially-challenged situation so that he could travel to swim meets and compete at the highest possible level. A picture of the swimmer displayed in his office was something that clients, prospective clients, staff members and wholesalers always spoke of. Another advisor helped with a portion of sponsorship to allow a high school class to go on a mission to a developing country and help build a small school. The picture of the students displayed in the advisor's office is something that virtually everyone gravitates to. Another advisor did a client event where he rented a movie theater for a screening of a Disney/Pixar film and the cost of admission for the kids was to bring a can of food for the local food bank. The picture of the kids standing beside the mountain of food outside the theater is a recurring topic of conversation in the office.

Socialize the Client Experience

Relationship building occurs outside your office, too.

Many top professional advisors interact socially with small groups of their favorite clients to stay connected, improve chemistry and stir the pot with clients. By design, they do so in a setting that is intriguing and memorable.

Whether it's arranging a small event at a Tesla dealership, a wine and cheese function at a museum, a Halloween evening at an old haunted mansion, a pseudo-antiques-road-show, vintage collector car fund-raising drive or a visit to a functioning farm, there are all kinds of intriguing events you can offer to get together with your clients to breathe some additional energy into your relationships. This clearly doesn't replace one-to-one conversations, lunches and get-togethers with clients, but one-to-many events can be a perfect complement.

When I say one-to-many, typically non-business functions should be kept on the smaller side. I've also seen many advisors offer virtual one-to-many conference calls, webinars and podcasts where they've interviewed subject matter experts, provide seasonally-themed events regarding tax changes, insights on selecting colleges and a host of other topics to larger audiences. If nothing else, from an intent and efficiency perspective, all of this falls under the category of good activity and can provide good optics and good productivity.

The *Law of Reciprocity* is powerful. When you bring a human touch to your business development effort and in the process express your gratitude to the community, you become more attractive and compelling to everyone you come in contact with.

There have been occasions where I've presented ideas like this at a seminar and some of the audience rolled their eyes to the point I felt like I was talking to slot machines. Always remember that you aren't marketing to yourself. At the end of the day you are in the relationship management business.

With the velocity of technology creeping into our lives accelerating, it's the human touch that stands out and gets people's attention. Don't get faked out by all the fancy and esoteric business-building ideas that sound good at a conference and then go to your head to die. Long-term relationships built on trust stem from your credentials as a professional advisor *and* the chemistry you build with your clients.

From my years of experience I can tell you this: The feedback loop on initiatives like this can be faster and more positive than anything else you do.

Secure Your Legacy While Enhancing Your Brand

Staying with the *Law of Reciprocity*, starting a foundation or charity can radically change your life both personally and professionally.

Of all of Mark Twain's famous quotes, this has to be among the most powerful: *"The two most important days of your life are the day you are born and the day you find out why."* He was referring, of course, to discovering your sense of purpose. As a professional advisor, discovering your sense of purpose can have a profound impact on your productivity and the personal fulfillment that comes from your role in the marketplace.

What were the primary reasons you became a professional advisor? What was your "Why"? Chances are it was to help people and make a good living.

You are in a unique position. You can earn a very respectable income as you make things better for a lot of people along the way. While I won't trivialize the importance of what you're earning, I will say that what matters is who you are becoming as a person as your life unfolds. That goes beyond the powerful S.W.A.N. acronym. Sure, you get to help people (and yourself) Sleep Well At Night, but go to the next level. Do you have any second-generation clients today? How about third-generation clients? If you don't now, someday you will be helping to secure multi-generational family legacies. That is powerful and not too many professions get to have that same impact.

Stephen Covey frequently asked his audiences to answer a question: *How will your life be defined*? When the time comes for your role as a professional advisor to wind down, how will you and those you have touched reflect on your contributions? Those are heavy questions to ponder, but here is the good news. No matter what stage you are at today, you can amplify your legacy and fulfillment to another level, starting right now, with one simple addition: Start a foundation or a charity or sponsor a community endeavor and subtly blend the messaging of your efforts in with your ongoing communication strategy.

In my travels I've come across several professional advisors, many of whom are clients of ours today, who have embraced this concept and have achieved a multitude of benefits as a result. From sponsoring a local athlete to organizing campaigns for the local food-bank to writing a book and donating the proceeds to a worthy cause, the stories of professionals giving back to the local or global community are awe-inspiring.

A Gimmick is Not Branding

I'm not suggesting for a moment that establishing a foundation or charity is a tactic or gimmick to drive business. The effort must be pure in-and-of-itself and stand on its own. That said, your efforts are a reflection of you and your philosophy, and give your clients, prospective clients and strategic partners something additional to connect with. Your team and your clients have something else to buy into as their relationship with you progresses. It speaks volumes about your community leadership and character. Your core skills and professional strategy are crucial to your success, but it's your character that strengthens relationships.

From a purely practical perspective, consider this: Marketing is what you say to the marketplace, while branding is how you are interpreted by the marketplace. If you are looking to enhance your brand and add to the fulfillment you realize from your job, I strongly encourage you to consider this concept.

Add Extra Meaning to Your Day-to-Day

I keep referring to fulfillment and I'll tell you why. As coaches to professional advisors, our goal is to help our clients restore liberation and order to their lives. Order stems from deploying best-practices that create consistency and predictability. Liberation stems from building a business that serves your life rather than the other way around.

While you can measure advisor productivity based on efficiency, profitability and other key metrics, it's the liberation and order factors that you *feel* the most. It's a huge commitment when you select a cause that you believe in strongly and decide to support it, but I'm convinced the R.O.I. is off the charts.

Since I've been passing along several quotes in this section, allow me to add one more by Marcus Cicero who in ancient Rome said, *"Ask not what your country can do for you, but rather what you can do for your country."* We all know the more popularized version of that quote, but the spirit is profound. I would humbly suggest a small modification: Ask what you can do for your community.

Whether it's locally or globally, the world will be a better place because of your efforts, and your level of rejuvenation and the improvement of your ability to "not sweat the small stuff" in life will be palpable.

Defining the Best

I touched on this earlier, but I want to cast this concept in a different light with a different example.

As a coach in the knowledge-for-profit community, I continually ponder this simple question: Why are some Professional advisors more effective than others?

You already know that the quality of your client relationships is just as important as the quality of your advice. And, as I've said, while I will never trivialize the importance of providing sound professional strategies and solid decision in the execution of them, they alone won't guarantee success. To reprise the checklist from earlier, there are three numbers in the combination that can unlock a professional advisor's full potential:

- **Core Solutions**
- **Practice Management**
- **Relationship Management**

To validate this, I often scrutinize what separates the best from the rest in this business. I look at why some advisors are more successful than others and what it is they are doing that others don't.

What's fascinating is that this study transcends the financial services industry. The most successful consultants, accountants and other skilled professionals aren't just effective at their core roles, they are also proficient at creating exceptional client experiences that lead to loyalty and refer-ability. The quality of the core deliverable is crucial, but that alone is not enough.

One of my favorite examples of the power of elevating the client experience and the power of positioning would have to be dentists, a group I touched on, earlier.

First Things First

One of the most important things dentists realized was that their time was their most valuable asset. As I've said, your dentist doesn't call you to confirm your next cleaning. Someone else does that. A good professional in any industry creates organization and structure and empowers people who make $25 per hour to do $25 per hour tasks. In the process this liberates the professional to focus on what he or she gets paid to do while creating scarcity that is attractive.

Master the Things That You Can Control

I reviewed the importance of controlling the controllable, earlier. Somewhere along their specific evolutionary curve, dentists also clued into the fact that their vocation was close to the top of the list of professions that people despised, and then they got smart and did something about it.

They started concentrating on the things that they could control.

One thing they could control was preparing an environment that was so memorable and relaxing that people felt comfortable. For the first time, people were talking about their dentists, and it wasn't in the context of pain. They were talking to their friends, families and colleagues about this special brand of 'instant rapport' that they had experienced, and it was at a dentist's office.

The *solution* a dentist provides isn't proprietary. The *experience* is. With that clarity on what is controllable, dentists ensure that clients buy into their process, instead of simply buying a commodity.

The other smart thing that successful dentists did was to help their patients map out a foundation for good dental health. As a part of this foundation, clients were taught that they would need regular and never-ending visits to the dentist to ensure that this strategy for good dental health was to succeed. In other words, it was an ongoing process that never ended until the patient died or lost their teeth. Clients are trained to *empower* their dentist.

Every new service provided by a dentist is communicated to clients in a forthright manner and positioned as a benefit to the client rather than as a sales opportunity. Clients become aware of their unmet needs before they even realize the need exists, and they take action.

Where is this all going? Is it such a stretch to think that we can implement the same kind of atmosphere and processes into the office of a professional advisor? Dentists realized that the overwhelmingly negative public predisposition toward their profession was out of their control, but that the client experience wasn't. Once they started mastering the office visit and educating their clients about the link between great dental health and how that was directly proportional to a lifelong relationship with their dentist, they have never looked back.

The good dentists attract, they don't chase.

Be Referable 365 Days a Year

Is it your fault as an advisor that the markets are volatile and the future is uncertain? Not any more than it's your fault when autumn becomes winter. Your responsibility, however, is that your clients are prepared for winter, and that it's not a shock to them when it arrives. However, if your clients tend to refer you only when things are rosy, you have a serious vulnerability in the way that you have positioned yourself. Things do not have to be this way!

If advisors would take a page or two from a profession that has already gone through this brand of disharmony, the dentists in the preceding section being a great example, they would finally have a business where clients can and will refer them regardless of how the markets are doing. This is not a pipe dream. There are advisors who have already integrated these things into their businesses. These advisors have clients who have been taught the doctrine and who are not faked out by volatility. As a result, because their clients' expectations have been exceeded in the areas that the advisor can control, these advisors are immensely referable 365 days out of the year.

When 'instant rapport' takes place at your office and the experience is coupled with a client process where the complexities of financial planning have been simplified and future-paced, clients will embrace your efforts. They will also realize that it would be a disservice not to recommend this five-star service to others they know who are unhappy with their professional advisors.

Through a crystal-clear client process, clients are taught that financial planning is not an event, but a process that involves ongoing interaction with their professional advisor, repeatedly and consistently as their lives and needs unfold.

Like the "dental health" mantra, clients can learn a financial mantra and will deliver it to others just as naturally and eloquently. With this kind of structure, to blame a professional advisor for an occasional or sustained hit to a balanced portfolio would be akin to blaming a dentist for your impacted wisdom tooth. The end result is that the instant rapport and the Client Process are what the clients learn to value in their dealings with the advisor, instead of fixating on the rate of return on their investments.

To those advisors who doubt the veracity of this claim, the number-one piece of feedback I hear from the clients of professional advisors who have embraced this approach of perfecting what they can control and improve on is: *"Finally! This is what we've been waiting for!"* Typically, when affluent prospective clients hear about a superior brand of advisor, they will distance themselves from the transaction-oriented advisor as quickly as possible and gravitate to the full-service advisor.

The bottom line is that everything – every action and reaction – executed by you and your team makes you either more or less referable. Scrutinize everything and create a referable experience so that you can nail down the small changes that makes for major improvement; the processes that sharpen the winning edge.

The Winning Edge

I believe we will see three primary types of professional advisors in the future: The robo/virtual advisor, salaried employees making a decent living, and elite entrepreneurial advisors processing their business through respected firms while making substantial incomes. I am convinced that financial services will remain an industry with strong income-earning potential, but that those who adapt to changes at a glacial pace will be left on the sidelines. We are entering into a Darwinian moment. Those who adapt will survive.

The *Winning Edge* is a fascinating premise with applications for these changes. In essence, the Winning Edge states that the disparities in the abilities of the best and the rest are often small, though the difference in rewards can be huge.

Let's use athletic endeavor as an analogy. At a recent US Open golf tournament, the winner Justin Rose collected $1.44 million in prize money. With a four-round total of 281, he earned about $5,124 every time he hit the golf ball. In the same tournament, runners-up Phil Mickelson and Jason Day, carded a four-round total of 283, only two strokes off of winner Justin Rose's total over 72 holes. Yet Mickelson and Day earned only (funny to have to say that) $696,000 each, or about $2,459 per shot. While Rose earned over twice as much as the second place finishers, was he more than twice as good? Clearly not.

The key quality inherent in professionals with the *Winning Edge* is entrepreneurship. In other words, they treat their business like a business. Many professional advisors regard an entrepreneur as a maverick, flying by the seat of his or her pants, living month-to-month to keep creditors at bay while trying to 'close' the next piece of business. True, a few of those exist, but my image of an entrepreneur, like those described in *E-Myth* or *The Millionaire Next Door*, is of the kind who runs his or her business like a well-oiled machine.

In the next five years, your industry will look very different, and more challenging, than it did five years ago. Professionals within every major industry have to understand these changes are constant and coming. We are well along that path now. One of the most important shifts you can make to thrive in the future is to adopt a systems-based approach to your business. This means that every process and activity you and your team execute on a daily basis is planned, scripted, refined and well-documented in a procedures manual.

The primary benefit of a systems-based operating approach is that you gain predictability and efficiency. Think of your business and marketing plan as a road map. Your operating manual serves as your GPS device. Not having this approach would be like walking through uncharted territory at night with only a flashlight for guidance. A good plan, one driven by systems, is like having a beacon five miles off, guiding you forward. It lets you see past short-term obstacles without drifting off-course.

Don't rely on hired talent. Become more talented by creating a systematic approach that you can hand to someone else to implement. You are truly on the verge of greatness when you have made yourself obsolete, and you are confident that your business would run faultlessly without you being there every day. It's not only liberating for the professional, it's rejuvenating, too.

There is much that you can't control and there is no sense worrying about any of that. Constantly scrutinize and refine the things you *can* control, especially when it comes to breathing life into your client relationships.

Your clients are your most valuable asset and you can't be complacent about your relationships with them.

Your clients' perception of you has been shaped by your rules of engagement and your code of conduct. You have effectively led them into a pattern of either focusing on what you cost and using you as a lightning rod to channel their frustrations or focusing on what you are worth and, in the latter case, the thought of defecting never occurs to them and the thought of endorsing you is always top of mind.

Demographics give you an Edge

If you have studied demography, you know that it is an incredible driver of trends and can influence your business, both sooner *and* later. American author Harry Dent and Canadian David Foote have written extensively about how large groups of people shift and how it impacts supply and demand – and thus your areas of control. Being conscious of demographics and integrating that knowledge with your process, refining and revisiting it as needed, is vital.

Demographic changes affect buying trends, consumerism and business in interesting ways. More coffee, tea or wine is consumed? Tooth whitening is suddenly an industry. Ear-buds are the standard? Audiology becomes a growth industry 20 years on.

We're not talking about disruptors that force sectors out of business like Blockbuster, here. The realities faced by Japan over the course of the last decade can be attributed in part to widespread demographic shifts. When you have more people retiring than you do entering the workforce, it creates incredible outcomes. In North America, imagine how the aging population will impact the real estate sector when it comes to the vast number of people unloading their second homes, not to mention downsizing from their large family homes? You have to believe that the extended care businesses, audiology and other health care sectors are well positioned in the future where other sectors that cater to younger buyers will struggle simply because that audience will be smaller in the future than it is now. In your business - as more people shift from their wealth accumulation years to their draw-down years and then to their transfer years - you will be impacted. Combined with commoditization and increasing volatility, you have to get out in front so that you aren't facing a collision course with obsolescence. You have to control what you can control.

Look at the concept of the robo-advisor. It commoditizes you in some respects, and think about its true addressable market. The generation that will inherit the wealth you currently manage is not about face time, it is about screen time. How many times have you seen your kids texting with a friend that is right beside them? How many times do you catch your kids watching a two- or three-minute YouTube video rather than reading a book or talking on the phone? In fact, I read recently on Bloomberg that current trends suggest that by 2020 robo-advisors will be "managing" two trillion dollars in assets. That's a lot of commas, and if you don't have relationships beyond the M of F.O.R.M. with the next generation, what do you think will happen?

10,000 is a Big Number: An Effective Approach for Attracting Soon-to-be Retired Clients

To return from the next generation to the current, let me focus on clients in transition. As more people head to the "back nine" (maybe yourself included) achieving a work-optional lifestyle, retiring without fear of outliving your money and family investment legacy planning become major motivations. Position yourself accordingly with clients shifting from accumulation to draw-down. If you're thinking about your own succession, who else could be more indispensable to a client who's going through succession planning issues than an advisor who has done their own? It gives you huge credibility on many levels.

Let's focus on your retiring clients. You have probably seen stories in the media of various mutual fund and asset management firms on both sides of the border referencing how many people retire every day. It has been estimated that, in America, 10,000 people enter retirement each day. That is a staggering number. Demographic realities like this create all kinds of new business opportunities, but the one that excites me most applies to professional advisors who are addressing this particular number with a client acquisition solution.

As you can imagine, during my travels as a speaker and consultant I come across countless examples of business development strategies used by professional advisors to attract retired or soon-to-be retiring clients. Without question, the most predictable and cost effective - not to mention most enjoyable - is hosting a retirement party for a newly-retired client.

The logistics are straightforward. When the advisor learns about an upcoming client retirement, he or she quietly contacts the client's spouse or significant other and offers to host the party. The spouse is responsible for invitations and RSVPs and the advisor is responsible for pulling the party together handing a turnkey event to the spouse.

As you know, people at retirement age tend to associate with, and live near, people much like themselves. This type of event creates a captive environment with high-quality MVPs. Because it's a low key, fun and celebratory event, people are open and casual. Once the word gets out to their friends that you were the driving force behind the retirement party, the goodwill and intrigue will create a frenzy of interest towards you.

When people start asking: "So I hear that you are Bob's professional advisor. What do you think about these markets?" avoid the rabbit-hole of fortune telling, or using a data-dumping elevator speech. Instead of making predictions, or describing yourself with a bland and interchangeable moniker like "We are Retirement Specialists", segue subtly into your value proposition and branding strategy using a hook and well packaged call to action:

"We work with affluent clients who are about five years or less from retirement. We've developed and refined an approach that helps our clients put all the pieces of the puzzle together to ensure they are prepared. We call it 'The Home Stretch Process'. Plus, we also like to have fun and celebrate our clients' achievements. If you'd like to learn more about our approach, give me your contact information and I'll have my assistant book an introductory conversation."

Again, as a professional, you are trying to attract new clients rather than chase them. When you explain that you have a process, you are positioned as an expert rather than as a salesperson.

The other benefit of this approach is that you will meet others within your client's family tree. In this situation, people closely connected to your retiring client get to see you, and connect with you, building important predisposition and mind-share. The children of your client will be inheriting these assets at some point down the road. If you are striving to establish second, third and even fourth generation clients, events like this can serve as a Trojan horse.

This is just one type of event you can hold to put yourself in a room with soon-to-be-retired and other prospective clients. Medicare-themed seminars and other educational events are common, as well.

Not to trivialize the value of education, but I'm reminded of Warren Buffet's quote "The marketplace will pay you more to entertain it than it will to educate it." Events that people can get excited about are the events that get moved up their priority list. Time is valuable and the options for how to spend time are countless. Do you really want to do another event that caters to the plate-lickers of the world?

An advisor asked my opinion about a lunch and learn seminar he was planning for clients and prospects. It sounded pretty boring, to be candid.

"I think your clients hire you to make all that stuff go away," I said. "They like knowing that you know what you're doing, but they don't need to know everything that you know. Why not call your event a barbecue, and that way good quality people will actually show up?"

Ultimately, you live by the rules you set. Events are great in terms of cause and effect; good activity will always lead to some productivity. The key is that the right people - including you and your team - get excited about the event. If you and your audience dread the idea, or can't see the value, the ROI will be far lower and the fulfillment factor will be zero.

Becoming a Fee-Worthy Advisor

I've talked about how, in this era of commoditization, more and more advisors come to me asking for help in ensuring their clients focus on what they are worth rather than what they cost. Especially at times when faced by a transition, whether of service, ownership or fee-structure.

The most predictable and effective way to execute a transition of any kind with your clients (the example given here being the shift from a commission-based compensation model to a fee-based model) is a three step re-framing process. With the need to make systemic transitions, knowing how to *not* lose clients in a given transition is vital.

Re-framing is essentially a process that enables you to communicate three things:

This is how things used to be

This is where we are today

This is the way things will be going forward

In all existing client relationships, people have a frame of reference defined by how you conduct yourself. Your objective, in keeping with the fact that change of any kind can stir up fear and uncertainty, is to clearly explain why you are doing it, how you are doing it and what it all means to them. The following three step re-framing process systematically addresses unspoken resistance and smooths the transition for both you and your clients.

Step 1 - The Ramp-up

Preparation is of paramount importance. To boil it down to the vital steps, you'll want to identify the following before you launch:

Master the Model - Completely internalize the platform you are choosing so that you can communicate its merits.

Identify the Clients - Choose the first wave of clients you will introduce the platform to.

Write out Scripts - Take the messaging out of your head and put it on paper so that you can rehearse and refine it and get comfortable with the flow.

Craft the Templates - Create meeting agendas and other visuals including a Panoramic Client Process (detailing your client service process) as well as a Critical Life Events document that emphasizes how a client's needs evolve as their life progresses.

Prepare the Tangibles - Create the initial meeting portfolio, the new/updated client welcome binder that will anchor the client to your new process and platform. Also order high quality thank-you cards and maintain a quantity on hand.

Step 2 - The Launch

Once the Ramp-up is complete, you can then begin the process of reaching out to your best clients to begin the transition process. Here are the steps to deploy:

Send the Intro Letter - This plants the seed for your professional evolution and sets the stage for the client.

Intro Call - This call books the first meeting to introduce the concept and get the client to begin buying into the process.

Initial Meeting - This agenda-based meeting introduces and outlines the concept and process of transitioning and sets the stage for the follow-up.

The Launching process is the moment of truth where clients get to contrast for themselves the distinctions between the old and new models (in this case a commission model and fee-based model). Explain the difference between buying investments and buying into a process and the merits of focusing on the value of advice versus the cost of transactions. Ultimately, you want the client to come to his or her own conclusions, and that is why no decisions or calls to action occur at this initial meeting.

Step 3 - The Follow-up

After the initial meeting, you tell the client that you will follow up in 48 hours to determine if there is a fit. Upon the client's buy-in, inform him or her that your assistant will call to set up the next meeting and the signing ceremony takes place at that time:

Onboard the Client - This agenda-driven meeting officially transitions the client to the platform.

Present the PFO Welcome Binder - This serves as the hub for the rest of the relationship and includes The Panoramic Client Process document and Critical Life Events document. These tools help to future-pace the client to help them stay connected to your process and ensure that they consistently view you as their personal CFO.

Communicate Your Introduction Process - Position the concept of you being a sounding-board for a friend or family member as a value-added service you are providing rather than as a favor you are requesting.

Send the Thank-you Card - Send a card that has impact and shelf-life and pay tribute to the fact that your relationship has enhanced and deepened.

REMAIN Fee-Worthy - You have set a new expectation for the client. It's one thing to succeed in the transition; it's another to maintain it now that the fees are transparent. You have to raise the bar in terms of your proactive and reactive service deliverables going forward. Keep in mind that stress and uncertainty live in the place between expectation and reality. If the service you provide meets or exceeds the expectations you've set, you maintain fee-worthiness, become indispensable to your clients and enhance your refer-ability in the process.

Keep a transition orderly, give the client clarity and an understanding of how the shift will benefit them and manage their expectations, and you will suffer few "lost in transition" clients.

If, on the other hand, you're at a stage where the transition you're contemplating is not to a new business model, but to a fishing shack on an exceptional trout lake, the next section will look at the ways you can bring order to your succession.

Bringing Success to Your Succession

I listed the top 10 goals of elite advisors, earlier. Those 10 goals should guide every step of a succession process. Recently, and prompted by demography, we have developed and refined a Succession 360 Process program that ensures a predictable outcome with a mentor and protégé.

From a demographic perspective, there are three distinct groups among the professional advisors I talk to on a regular basis. There are the 50-and-up advisors who are looking down the road at the eventual sale of their business. These advisors have been in the business a long time, achieved a high level of success, and are now three to five years out from transitioning to the next chapter in their lives.

There are the 30-ish advisors who are extremely ambitious and want to light the afterburner in terms of growing their respective business. These advisors don't want to rely solely on organic growth, they want to acquire a business (or two), ideally from someone who has patiently and methodically built a durable practice and is looking to exit.

Finally, there are the advisors somewhere in between who want to remain in the business but have a unique view on succession. Rather than sell, they want to leverage their momentum *and* plan for the future by grooming an associate (often a second generation of the family) or partner with an advisor, be it a junior or equal. While there is no specific timetable for succession, this advisor gets to create some scale, liberate time to focus solely on top clients, and create options for the future in the meantime.

In each scenario, the key is to multiply the outcome and there are specific steps that can be taken to add precision to the process and predictability to the results.

Partnering is Not for Everyone

In the traditional partnering scenario there are countless examples of success, mediocrity and failure.

The shining examples of success stem from an emphasis on fit and process. The also-rans stem from a lack of true synergies and the only real alignment of interest was to enhance the payout until the older partner transitioned out of the business. The worst examples tend to be a $500k advisor partnering with another $500k advisor and in time the combined revenue became $800k. Those stem from a lack of preparation, incompatibility, and poor execution. For those advisors, 1+1 = 1.5 and with the merge came an increase in overhead and hassle-factor.

In the case of partnering with a junior advisor, especially someone related to the lead advisor, it is essential that the protégé understand the following:

- *Success goes beyond rates of return*. Success is as much about relationship management as it is about asset management.

- *Run the business like a business*. Following predetermined and documented procedures creates a consistent client experience ensuring the conversion of clients to advocates.

- *There are no free rides*. The junior advisor needs to generate meaningful and measurable client acquisition and business development results from their own efforts.

Too many mentors leave the protégé to their own devices to figure things out. You can't play to maverick talent; you have to play to process.

The most successful advisors to partner with a second-generation or junior created, essentially, a franchise-ready environment. This not only freed the mentor to focus on the top 20 percent of clients, knowing that the 80 percent were well taken care of by the protégé, it created the sense of an upgrade for clients rather than feeling like they'd been handed-off, resulting in uncovering untapped new business opportunities along the way .

There are countless examples of successes, anticlimactic outcomes and outright failures in the acquisition world. The old model came down to the buyer focusing on what the business would *cost*, while the seller was fixated on what the business was *worth* with little emphasis placed on the key intrinsic and proprietary assets. There was also little thought applied to deploying a turnkey and proven process to communicate with the clients involved prior to, during, and after the transition.

Many knowledge-for-profit professionals who buy or sell a practice are only buying a book of business, not an actual business. There are several key performance indicators that go beyond the trailing 12. So what is the difference between a 1X transaction and a 2X or better multiplied transaction?

One of the most important issues is the quality of the client relationships. That is just as important as the quantity of total assets. How loyal are the clients based on how they have been served up to this point in the relationship? Have they bought investments, or are they bought-into a professional process? Metrics on empowerment, referrals, demographics and commonalities, commissions vs. fees and several other issues are key as well.

The bottom line is this: Whether you plan to buy or sell a business in the future, it is essential that you get out front and be well-prepared to multiply the value of the asset and make the outcome as smooth and predictable as possible.

Deploying a process demystifies the experience and ensures there is minimal opportunity leakage - and that you don't squander your time.

There are more Sellers than Buyers

As a seller, when you tighten up your business through organization and structure as well as essential best practices, you unlock hidden value that differentiates you from others with similar aspirations. In 12 months or less you can execute a panoramic practice management process that a suitor will recognize as extremely valuable.

Remember what a buyer wants: Only pleasant surprises. They want the transition to be smooth, and the integration into their core business to be virtually effortless.

Acquire a Real Asset, Not Just a Collection of Assets

As a buyer, there are many tangible and intangible issues to address in your due-diligence process. The key is to look for a business that has been built on a foundation of predictable, sustainable and duplicable processes, especially as it relates to service and relationship management. Again, the quality of the relationships, driven by the expectations they have and the experience they've received, will have a profound impact on relationship durability and untapped potential going forward.

Many buyers in the past have acquired sketchy books thinking there was a vein of gold or all kinds of low-hanging fruit just waiting to be uncovered. As a result, the buyer was fixated on the price of the acquisition rather than the quality of the asset, resulting in an outcome that spiraled downward.

Quality relationships last long after you pay for them. Get clarity on the issues that will impact your transaction and be organized with a plan and a process. As a potential seller, the longer you wait and the less prepared you are, the less value you will get from your asset. As a buyer, the longer you wait and less prepared you are, the more revenue and momentum you will forgo. In both cases, the dollars you make will be lower, and in both cases the hassle factor and frustration will be higher.

Preparation will help you squeeze more juice out of the orange.

For years we've been reminding advisors that one of the primary qualities that separate the best from the rest isn't in what someone knows, but rather in their commitment to well-thought-out action. Knowledge is being *aware* of something, but wisdom is understanding how to *act* on something. We've seen, time and again, advisors who know what they should be doing, but who simply don't act. Common sense isn't always a common practice.

Knowledge is knowing a tomato is a fruit. Wisdom is not putting it in a fruit salad - Miles Kingston

---

There are universal issues that apply to both the buyer and seller when it comes to identifying an alignment of interests between two advisors. I'll be following a dual track as I address these issues so that they apply to both parties.

Don't Get Faked Out

From a philosophical perspective, one of the most important qualities of an advisor is having a mindset that says: "My goal is not to see how big I can get, but rather how small I can stay." That sounds like a contradiction from a buyer's perspective. Why else would someone want to buy a business other than to grow in a hurry?

It's still a great idea to accelerate growth through acquisition, but the focal point should be on the quality of the clients, not the quantity. An advisor who was disciplined in only attracting clients who were a good fit, rather than accepting anyone with a pulse, is the ideal advisor to purchase a business from. The same holds true in terms of selling a business to an advisor with a similar mindset because, ultimately, you know your clients will be transitioned and onboarded professionally and will enjoy a soft landing, thus ensuring the seller's legacy in the process.

A professional who tends to consistently attract the same type of clients in terms of average asset size and other commonalities is another item on the ideal alignment checklist. The average value of a client and the platform they are on is more important than the overall amount of assets the selling professional has.

As a specific note to financial advisors, for a variety of reasons it is a good idea to attempt to align with an advisor within the firm. That's not to say that there can't be exceptions, but the clients have a degree of comfort and familiarity with the firm's systems and procedures, and there will be fewer disruptions in terms of trust, optics and deliverables which contributes to the clients' confidence in the transition.

How Did They Start Relationships?

The ideal financial services professional uses a fit process rather than a sales process. They use many of the processes I've covered in this book. They don't try to convince someone to become a client; they establish an alignment between the person's needs and the advisor's solutions. Their clients are enlightened and in sync with the advisor's mindset about wealth management. Good questions to uncover that congruency are:

- What is the client acquisition history in terms of referral genealogy?

- What percentage of clients were referred from the 20 percent who generate 80 percent of the business vs. from the 80 percent who generate just 20 percent of the business?

- What percentage of their business was organically acquired vs. absorbed from within the branch or acquired by purchase?

- Were cold-calling, mass marketing and seminars used to acquire clients?

- What percentage of their clients are actually partial customers who dabble with other providers vs. fully empowering advocates?

- What is their process to communicate their services professionally to consistently attract new money as it goes into motion?

- Do they have meaningful "two-way street" relationships with accountants, lawyers and other partners?

The answers to these questions will help you determine what the real value of a book of business is, and whether there is a fit with your own goals.

Entering the Retirement or Acquisition Red-Zone

When I coach an advisor about performing solid due-diligence on a potential buyer or seller, a common response is "This sounds like work!"

It is, but use the potential of a multiplied ROI as the beacon that helps you see past the hurdles and noise that will try to conspire against you.

Much of the value of the business you are trying to acquire or sell is intangible and abstract, especially if it isn't defined or documented. Get out in front of the process, get your intellectual properties out of your head, and subscribe to the maxim that says *Done is Better than Perfect*. Invest your time in a process and put the odds in your favor. We've seen first-hand where an advisor invested 6 to 12 months of sweat equity into the business to position it to be sold and then multiplied their outcome meaningfully. We've also seen how a well-prepared acquisition and methodical transition multiplied the profitability of the combined practice.

Whether buying or selling, deploy a process, execute it with precision and you will unlock more value.

The Multiplier Method: Creating Your Ideal Life through Expanding, Enhancing or Exiting

Life is full of lessons that come in the form of examples and warnings; examples of things done properly, and warnings where errors in judgment were made.

The most effective people in virtually all fields of endeavor study and assimilate both the lessons of adversity through mistakes (external forces) and adversity engendered by misconduct (internal forces). Learning from that information creates predictable outcomes for themselves in the future.

One example I like to share, and that can be learned from when it comes to multiplying the value of a financial services business, can be found in real estate. You'll recognize it from the *Let's Shoot Your Trailer* section at this book's outset.

When you sell a home, it's a good idea to hire a professional to stage it so a prospective buyer can see the home in its ideal form. Often a small staging investment can lead to an accelerated sale and amplified price. Whatever the future holds for you as you strive to move in the direction of your Ideal Life, the staging mindset should be applied well in advance so that you are out in front and well-prepared.

The beauty of this approach is that it provides you with many benefits beyond just buying and selling. Every week I speak with advisors who tell me what's next for them in terms of actualizing specific goals. These goals include:

- Achieving the next level of productivity and client acquisition.
- Transitioning to the next generation for a smooth internal succession.
- Pursuing the next challenge in life by right sizing and taking a few marbles off the table.
- Shifting to the next gear of efficiency and profitability through structure and process.
- Moving to the next chapter in life by exiting the business or switching firms.

The preceding list outlines just a few of the goals I hear on a regular basis. Whatever your Ideal Life looks like in your mind, there will be many moving parts that will require a holistic view on planning and preparation that will include:

Depersonalizing the business – To ensure that it runs like a Swiss watch whether or not you are there.

Developing and refining procedures - To create predictable and sustainable outcomes.

Documenting your procedures - To fully maximize your intellectual and proprietary assets.

Success in Buying or Selling a Business comes by Design, not by Chance

I'd like to provide an overview of the three-step process used when executing the transition. After you have established a fit, based on an alignment of interests between buyer and seller, you then shift your focus to deploying a communication process to transition clients. Properly done, the seller will have multiplied the value of his or her business, and the buyer will predictably multiply his or her profitability and overall ROI by capitalizing on untapped opportunities.

1. **The Ramp-up** - Being prepared up-front with a methodical transitional process that will build predisposition and buy-in for the clients involved.

2. **The Launch** - A sequential approach to communicate the process to clients and position it as a benefit and service to them.

3. **The Follow-through** - How to fast-track clients to advocate status and uncover untapped business through an empowerment process.

Do those three steps sound familiar? They should. The core processes you apply to transitioning clients from the *Becoming Fee-Worthy* section apply here, though with a different perspective.

Before I provide the overview, I want to spend a moment on one of the most overlooked aspects of the buying and selling process. I'm referring to how the concept is positioned, communicated and perceived by the clients involved.

Client relationships are among the most valuable proprietary assets in the sectors occupied by professional advisors, but it is common for advisors to be fixated on the asset level of *"The Book"* and the financial aspects of the transaction. Many overlook or trivialize the emotional impact on the client. This isn't even always a conscious issue. The buyer focuses on the assets and potential revenue stream but not as much on relationship issues. The seller focuses on the asset value being sold but not as much on the legacy issues involved.

If you want to multiply the outcome and minimize the anticlimactic issues that can stem from this, you have to take a panoramic view.

Client Perception and Buy-in are Critical

The bottom line is this: The transitional process has to be positioned and communicated as a benefit to the clients involved so that they don't feel like pawns in a transaction.

The investment world is all about confidence and trust. Whether you are buying or selling, the more effectively and consistently you communicate with the clients involved, the more you will multiply the value of what you are buying or selling.

Let's go back to the three-step process of ramp-up, launch and follow-through.

1. The Ramp-up

The objective in the initial phase of the process is to create comfort and predisposition among the client base. I've seen many transactions in the past where the buyers and sellers did not get out in front of the client communication process to be well-prepared to create awareness and clarity before the transition occurred.

You can't wing it and hope for the best. You need to have a clearly defined track to give you scale, efficiency and predictability. If clients are neglected, their imaginations can run wild and they will come to their own conclusions as to what this event will mean to them.

Depending on the numbers of clients involved, you may need a one-to-many process to address the B and C clients along with a one-to-one process for the A clients. Many sellers will stage the transition and retain some key clients through a protected list, making the Ramp-up process that much more important in terms of multiplying the value.

It takes time to put this together. I often recommend a six- to 12-month ramp-up so that clients are well prepared and don't feel the transition is being sprung on them.

As a foundational kick-start, a call rotation and increase in proactive service is deployed, including a F.O.R.M. gathering process. Client classification tied to a service matrix is essential for clarity. Implementing a Personal Financial Organizer (PFO) process so that clients are aware of the full array of services provided is also an important step. Tangible tools such as Introductory Kits and using agendas in review meetings help take the business from vapor to paper and amplify professionalism. A client advisory council and other seed-planting steps about future client service enhancements are also very effective.

2. The Launch

As you segue from the Ramp-up to the actual transition, a re-framing process is a major piece of the puzzle to ensure the rubber hits the road smoothly. Essentially, what you are doing is saying "this is how things used to be, this is how things are today, and this is what you can expect going forward."

Clients have an expectation and frame of reference based on the relationship they've had up to this point. It's essential to roll out the process so that they view this as an enhancement and benefit to them.

Change is not always embraced easily by people. The transitional process has to ensure a soft landing so that clients are competitor-proof and focus on what you are worth rather than what you cost.

3. The Follow-through

Once the transition has been formally put into motion, it is essential that the buyer and seller have a predictable and sustainable process in place to meet and exceed the expectations set for the clients involved.

For the seller, the transaction has been multiplied up-front but the focus now shifts to legacy. For the buyer, the concept of multiplying the value of the clients acquired is just starting.

The transitional onboarding steps, and the ability to uncover new business and fast track clients to advocate status, can be achieved predictably using a sequential communication process. As I've said before, this isn't a transactional approach where you are getting someone to agree with a change in their reality. Nor is the transition accomplished with a simple announcement process; it is sequential and it blends into your service model to ensure consistency. You want them to buy into the transition as an enhancement to their lives to the point that they feel compelled to empower you more and endorse you to others. This takes time and it requires a process.

Those who are prepared and patiently roll out a communication plan will maximize their new and existing client relationships and multiply the value of their asset.

In school, you're taught a lesson and then given a test. In life, you're given a test that teaches you a lesson - Tom Bodett

The Advisor Flight Plan: Taking the Mystery Out of the Next Chapter of Your Life

One of my favorite questions to ask a professional advisor during a gap analysis early in the year is "Where do you see yourself in the next 5 years?"

The holiday period encourages most people to contemplate not only what they are grateful for, but also what they aspire to as they launch into the New Year. As you can imagine, I hear all kinds of W-5 responses from advisors. But, more and more often, some of the best advisors in the business tell me that they are considering moving from their current firm to one that is a better fit for them, and for their clients.

Avoiding the Epic Fail

Because many advisors have switched firms in the past and the experience was more difficult than anticipated, and the outcome anticlimactic because the grass wasn't any greener, there can be a lot of anxiety about the process. In the spirit of *Beginning with the End in Mind*, you ultimately want your next move to be your last move, and accordingly you will want to get out in front of all the related issues and check every single box to ensure the outcome is even better than you hoped for.

It's All About Fit

The move must be positioned as a benefit to your clients, and in doing so, it reflects well on you as their advisor. The process of defining and identifying an ideal environment so that this can, in fact, be the last move you ever make should revolve around these benchmarks for your target firm:

- The firm is client-centric and has a culture of service.
- The firm appreciates stewardship over salesmanship.
- The firm goes beyond window-dressing when it comes to advisor best practices.
- The firm walks-the-talk using systems and procedures to ensure consistency and efficiency.
- The firm understands that client relationships are just as important as product performance.

Once those issues are settled to your satisfaction, you can look at putting together your next step.

The Pre-Flight Checklist

Even the most seasoned pilot will review his or her pre-flight checklist prior to departure. Though they could probably take off in their sleep, they still refer to the list to ensure nothing has been missed.

I want advisors to expect the best while being prepared for the worst so that they experience an uneventful departure, are positioned to address any unforeseen turbulence, and are ready for a smooth landing. In the following I'll be sharing several strategies to ensure you can:

- Be crystal clear about the why so that your clients will see the merit and buy into the change.
- Have a clearly defined and methodical approach to make the transition.
- Deploy a process that not only ramps up and executes, but also follows-through over the long haul.
- Reset client relationships in a way that positively re-frames how they perceive and empower you.

Expectation management for yourself and your clients is vital. The stronger your relationships are, and the better your communication strategy and execution is, the more likely that your clients will say to you, "Whatever you think is best. I will follow you anywhere."

A checklist ensures that nothing is overlooked. It activates the process of ensuring your clients perceive you as a professional with a process, and helps them favorably contrast you to any pretenders who try to lure them away. While not complete, the following is a good start to build your own:

- Get it all out of your head: F.O.R.M. and Know Your Client data, service procedures, etc.
- Start using agendas in all meetings.
- Refine your onboard and review process with Personal Financial Organizers.

249

- Articulate your value proposition with a personal branding strategy.
- Competitor-proof clients with a service matrix.
- Reintroduce yourself and your team with a re-framing process.
- Communicate the value of the message and the messenger.

By tangibly enhancing the client experience, you raise the bar and create a new frame of reference that elevates you above the pack. It deepens the connection and ensures your clients are predisposed to loyalty to you.

Expectation Management

I've repeatedly said that stress, disappointment and anxiety are born in the place between expectation and reality. If you expect something to go a certain way and there is a gap between that expectation and reality, stress will appear. You can close that gap and experience a positive outcome through methodical preparation and execution. When you check all the boxes on your pre-flight checklist, you are cleared for departure and can expect a smooth flight.

Dispelling Myths and Misconceptions

Of all the benefits that come from having a third party like myself work with an advisor well in advance of a switch from one firm to another, the most important are helping the advisor focus on what matters most, and instilling the sense of confidence that comes from preparation and organization.

A component of this stems from dispelling myths and misconceptions, and addressing areas of uncertainty that can consume the advisor long before they even select their next home.

Many advisors I talk to have switched firms in the past and the transitional experience wasn't a positive one. As the nagging feeling sets in that they should consider their options going forward, fears creep in as they reflect on past errors and unexpected problems that appeared. They want to get it right and make sure this is the last move they ever make. They also want to make sure the hassle factor is reduced and the benefits are amplified.

The following three common misconceptions stem from frequent conversations I've had with advisors who revealed their mindset as they contemplated their future:

It Will Work Because it HAS to! Hope is not a strategy. This will work because you're organized.

If Some is Good, More is Better! A move is a perfect opportunity to right-size, re-set and re-frame existing relationships.

This Will Be Complicated and Overwhelming! This can be smooth and productive if you're prepared.

Keep it Simple: Make the Hole Bigger

As I address these three issues, let me first tell you one of my favorite marketing stories. It reinforces the message that you should keep things simple, focusing on what matters most and is within your control. The story centers on Tabasco sauce and the company's push to sell more product.

In an effort to drive up sales, Tabasco supposedly asked their employees for suggestions. Without question, the most intriguing idea brought forward was not expensive, esoteric or abstract. It was simple.

Make the hole bigger and the speed of consumption would increase.

Ultimately I don't know if Tabasco acted on the idea or whether the story is fictitious, but what I do know is that often the best idea is both obvious and elegantly simple.

If you are familiar with Occam's Razor, you know that the best solution to any problem or issue is usually the simplest. When it comes to the issue of switching from one firm to another, the same holds true: Keep it simple, get way out in front, and focus on the most important asset you have - client relationships.

It doesn't have to be complicated.

Strengthen Relationships Before You Select a Firm

Long before you've decided on the right firm to move to, based on your ideal culture and environment criteria, and before you create your pre-departure checklist of all your logistical boxes to check off, you have to take a good hard look at your existing client relationships and whether or not your clients are as deeply connected to you as they should be.

We've seen firsthand how an advisor can become bogged down with the noise and issues of a transition (or just the day-to-day job) and, in the process, neglect their clients or take them for granted.

Everything you do is either important or essential. Strengthening client relationships is the most essential thing you do, regardless of whether or not change is on the horizon.

A Change of Heart

An interesting outcome often emerges when an advisor takes the steps I outline to strengthen their client relationships; their intent to move diminishes. They realize that, when they focus on what they can control, where they hang their hat is often secondary. I've helped just as many advisors stay where they are as I have to move.

That being said, there are many other advisors who have outgrown their existing firms and believe that they and their clients would be better served in a new environment. The key is to take the long view and approach all this in a patient, methodical and sequential manner.

Cleared for Departure

Too many advisors hit the wall with their existing firm, get fed up, and then make a quick, emotional decision to switch. At that point the gravity and magnitude of the situation sets in and they get anxious about how their clients will respond to the news.

That is putting the cart before the horse and will put you into the mindset of *"It will work because it HAS to."* Like Cortez burning the boats to create commitment from his troops, showing them that they had no option but to win the battle because there was no plan B, now the advisor is desperate and has to scramble.

Good decisions stem from strong positions. When you deploy a strategy to strengthen relationships well in advance, you are operating from a position of strength.

A fallacy exists that suggests you must grow or perish: *"If Some is Good, MORE is better."* As you have read, I often tell advisors that the goal is not to see how big you can get, but rather how small you can stay.

One of the greatest benefits of moving to an environment that is better suited to your core philosophy is that it is also a tremendous opportunity to disassociate from certain clients that are not a good fit for you going forward. It also gives you the opportunity to re-frame your remaining relationships so that your clients fully understand and appreciate your value to them.

By creating an ideal client profile, sticking to it ardently and disassociating from clients that don't fit, you reinforce the perception that the move will be a benefit to the client in terms of service and stewardship, while creating an aspirational environment where you attract great clients rather than accepting anyone with a pulse.

A move can be *overwhelmingly complicated and stressful* if you have not considered the full spectrum of issues, and if you are not prepared.

Again, client relationships are, and will always be, your most valuable asset, and the issues related to strengthening those relationships have to be at the top of your list. If you have done your homework, and communicated your process to your clients, your move can be predictable and smooth.

Knowledge is Everywhere

As I eased into the chair at the shoe shine booth, I half-jokingly asked the man if he could make my tired shoes look new again. To my surprise, he answered, "You have to do a lot of things for your shoes long before you get them shined if you want to keep them looking like new."

What followed was a five minute clinic on shoe maintenance.

"First," he told me, "you have to get cedar shoe trees. Put them in your shoes each night and they'll prevent them from looking like Ali Baba's. Second, buy some lanolin cream like the stuff I'm using right now and apply it every couple of weeks. That will keep the leather soft and moist, prevent cracking and stop embedded creases from developing."

All the while, as the lesson continued, he performed what was the most efficient and skilled shoe polishing I had ever experienced. I was told to only buy shoes with thick soles, since thin soles don't look as "strong or confident", and to use lace-up shoes only for business, as well as a number of other helpful tips.

So why am I sharing this with you? Because everything is a study, and knowledge is everywhere; even at the foot of a shoe-shine chair.

Learn by Formal Study, Learn by Being Aware

One of my favorite business philosophers, Jim Rohn, told me that a formal education will help you earn a living, while continual self-education can make you rich. It is true that income rarely exceeds self-development.

While a professional advisor's CE credits generally revolve around building their credentials, that is only one piece of the puzzle. Your success also depends on your ability to develop chemistry with clients, and that is a study as well. Don't just study the markets, study marketing.

Many life skills and qualities lead to you being attractive to the marketplace. Self-development shapes your character and philosophy. Appropriately enough, the word 'philosophy' stems from the Greek for *love of knowledge*. If you took it upon yourself to read one book a month on business development strategies, you would be in an elite group within this industry.

The less people know, the more stubbornly they know it - Osho

Look Inward at your Existing Clientele to Find What Works Best

Don't stop at reading books. Study your existing business. How did you attract your favorite clients? I'm astounded when advisors engage in time consuming tactics such as seminars, direct mail campaigns, trade shows and cold calling, although none of their best clients were attracted in these ways. Replicate your best successes.

If you track your client genealogy and discover that your best clients were referrals or introductions, invest your time and money in that area.

Turn Common Sense into Action

As a practice management and business development consultant, I often hear clients say that they like our information because it's creative; in truth, it is often not about creativity. Our clients are our best teachers, and their experiences help us help others navigate through their challenges (If they hit us up for royalties, we're sunk.)

We are constantly asked for new ideas. Here's another truth: There are very few new ideas, simply existing approaches that are refined and customized for one's own situation.

So look around and pay attention.

Network and befriend other top advisors. They have knowledge and, most of the time, they are prepared to share it with you.

This final section has largely been a collection of gentle reminders of things you already know. Sometimes you just need to hear them again. As Confucius said, "when the student is ready, the teacher will appear." But don't delay and let the *Law of Diminishing Intent* rob you of the wealth of skills that stem from being a serious student.

Now would be a perfect time to get busy.

From Intent to Implement: Why "Done" is better than "Perfect"

Of the many universal laws and principles that affect us all in life, the one that intrigues me the most is the aforementioned *Law of Diminishing Intent*.

In life, the pendulum often swings between ambition and contentment. Ultimately we want to savor what we have while continually striving to achieve our full potential. Many of us set goals in late December or early January as we strive to achieve new levels of personal and professional success in the coming year, and while our ambition and self-motivation may be strong, the velocity of life can be so intense that distractions and noise compete for our attention and conspire against our initiative. This pushes our goals off to the side and eventually right out our minds.

The Bottom Line is this: Change is Hard

Let's revisit Aristotle's maxim, here: "Quality is a habit, not an act. We are what we repeatedly do."

We are products of our habits and rituals. Creating a new habit can be difficult because traction and meaningful results take time to manifest. Our daily routines get hardwired into our mindset and whenever we deviate we often subconsciously revert back to our original ways of doing things.

An important step is to develop an approach where you take action and build the bridge as you cross it. If you know you have to start doing something that's in your best interest or, for that matter, stop doing something that is *not* in your best interest, take action and let the momentum of your new habit compound over time.

If you know that you should be doing an ongoing call rotation or send out birthday cards to your best clients, but you never get around to it, start with a small number of 10 or 20 clients. Calling 100 clients every 60 days can seem ominous, but calling 20 seems easy. Once you get into a rhythm of consistency you can increase the numbers.

Follow the process and, as the results become obvious, you will be motivated to not only expand the process but to also continue with it.

Minor Adjustments Can Lead to Major Improvements

The *Law of Cause and Effect* suggests that our ongoing activities determine our productivity.

We have to identify the actions we need to take on a regular basis that contribute to our overall effectiveness. Now, apply that along with The Pareto Principle. If 80 percent of our productivity stems from 20 percent of our activities – meaning we make 80 percent of our income in about an hour a day – we have to identify, master and continuously deploy the activities that matter the most. These habits and rituals make up our code-of-conduct that earns the trust of our clients, leads to predictable results, and impacts our branding in terms of how we are perceived by everyone we interact with.

Talk really is cheap. Actions really do speak louder than words. The key is in constantly refining those actions so that we aren't mistaking movement for achievement.

What's the Worst That Can Happen?

There is another reason why we don't take action and develop a new habit before our intent diminishes: Fear. As easy as it is to change, it's always easier not to if there is uncertainty or risk.

I talk to advisors about this all the time and I often share my personal view on how I try to overcome the core issues that lead to procrastination. I continually remind myself that life is short and I don't want to be defined by my fears of failure. I'm also driven by the fact that my sense of purpose and fulfillment in life stems from the fact that the things that cause me anxiety or stress are never as big as they appear.

Furthermore, ultimately I am one of seven billion people on earth. I'm just a small speck in the grand scheme of things. Don't get me wrong, I have a strong self-esteem but it does help to keep things in proportion. I read recently that NASA estimates that there are probably 40 billion planets about the size of the Earth in our galaxy alone, orbiting in the "Goldilocks zone" – not too hot, not too cold - that allows for the possibility of life. That gives me the perspective not to major in minor things and motivates me to take action and live a little. Sure, I want to be rational and prepared, I want to use sound judgment in my planning, but I refuse to let the fear of failure shackle me.

Regret is always a possibility but I want to approach life looking forward at what could be rather than looking back at what could have been.

If you are a fan of reading biographies of high achievers, you know that the people who are the most gratified as they reflect back on life are those who took action, overcame adversity and lived life to the fullest.

I'll never trivialize the importance of knowledge but it's the reputation of *action* that creates the most interesting legacies. What we know will never matter more than our results. Knowledge isn't power. Knowledge invested in action is power, and by acting you become an inspiration for others and leave an indelible mark on the world.

So let's all be brave, be relentless, and be patient for results to appear as we take action throughout the year.

Do it for what it makes of you, not just for what it gets you. It's not what you get in life that makes you valuable, it's who you become that really matters the most - Jim Rohn

---

Visit **www.TheAdvisorPlaybook.com** for access to the Playbook Implementation Program

paretosystems
Consistent. Results.

Coaching Professional Advisors for Over 20 Years

Achieve Success through Proven Process

Pareto Systems coaches successful knowledge-for-profit professionals in many fields including financial advisors, insurance specialists and estate-planning attorneys on practice management and client acquisition.

To learn more about advisor solutions, contact us:

paretosystems.com   **1.866.593.8020**

 Overcome
Your Plateau

 Achieve Consistent
Client Acquisition

 Elevate Your Client
Experience

 Create a Professional
Branding Strategy

The Multiplier Method	1:1 Coaching	Business Evaluation Process Gap Analysis
Succession Planning	Advisor Flight Plan	Transitioning to Fee-Based

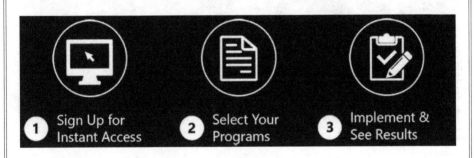

Total Client Engagement (TCE)

A 7 Step Process to Become Their Personal CFO

Duncan MacPherson, CEO of Pareto Systems, has developed and refined an actionable proven process that enables you to quickly and predictably:

- **Competitor-Proof Clients**
- **Gain Their Full Empowerment**
- **Create Referral-Generating Advocates**

This turnkey process can plug and play into:
Your current on-boarding process to fast track to empowerment and advocacy, and your current client review process to reframe and maximize existing relationships

This is what you get:
Three linked and sequential consultations to ensure implementation
Access to all scripts, tools and templates
Resources to ensure clients identify with the people, the practice and the process

You will:
De-commoditize your core solutions
De-personalize and professionalize the client experience
De-mystify how you are perceived and described

Reduce friction, improve the enterprise value of your business by deepening your relationships – effortlessly! Contact us to learn more:

1.866.593.8020 ext 1211
inquiries@paretoplatform.com

paretosystems
Consistent. Results.

CPSIA information can be obtained
at www.ICGtesting.com
Printed in the USA
BVHW072148211019
561687BV00002B/4/P

9 780968 440186